MAN AND THE WORLD
OF STARS

THE SPIRITUAL
COMMUNION
OF MANKIND

MAN AND THE WORLD
OF STARS
THE SPIRITUAL
COMMUNION
OF MANKIND

RUDOLF STEINER

Twelve Lectures delivered at Dornach,
November-December, 1922

Translation by D. S. OSMOND

ANTHROPOSOPHIC PRESS, INC.

NEW YORK

Translated from shorthand reports unre-
vised by the lecturer. The title of the vol-
ume in the Complete Centenary Edition
containing the German original of these
lectures is: *Das Verhaeltnis der Sternenwelt zum Menschen und des Menschen zur
Sternenwelt.—Die geistige Kommunion
der Menschheit.*

2nd printing 1982
ISBN 0-88010-008-7

Cover design by Peter Van Oordt

This translation has been authorized for
the western hemisphere by agreement with
the Rudolf Steiner Nachlassverwaltung,
Dornach, Switzerland.

PRINTED IN THE UNITED STATES OF AMERICA

In his autobiography, *THE COURSE OF MY LIF.* (chapters 35 and 36), Rudolf Steiner speaks as follows concerning the character of this privately printed matter:

"The content of this printed matter was intended as oral communications, not to be printed. . . .

"Nothing has ever been said that is not in utmost degree the purest result of the developing Anthroposophy. . . . Whoever reads this privately printed material can take it in the fullest sense as containing what Anthroposophy has to say. Therefore, it was possible without hesitation . . . to depart from the plan of circulating this printed matter among members alone. Only, it will be necessary to put up with the fact that erroneous matter is included in the lecture reports which I did not revise.

"The right to a judgment about the content of such privately printed material can naturally be conceded only to one who knows what is taken for granted as the prerequisite basis of this judgment. And for most of this printed matter prerequisite will be *at least* the Anthroposophical knowledge of the human being, and of the cosmos, to the extent that their nature is set forth in Anthroposophy, and of what exists in the form of 'Anthroposophical history' in the communications from the world of spirit."

These twelve lectures were given in the main auditorium of the first Goetheanum in Dornach, Switzerland. As Rudolf Steiner was writing the two verses of the last lecture on the blackboard, on December 31, 1922, a fire was already smoldering in the south wing of the building between the double wooden walls. A few hours later the Goetheanum had burned to the ground.

CONTENTS

MAN AND THE WORLD OF STARS

I

The Spirit-Seed of Man's Physical Organism. Walking, Speaking and Thinking, and Their Correspondences in the Spiritual World.

Dornach, November 26, 1922

THESE lectures will deal with the two states of life through which man passes: in the spiritual world between death and a new birth, and in the physical world between birth and death.

I want to remind you today of certain matters to which your attention was directed in recent lectures here. I said that during the very important period stretching between death and a new birth, man finds himself in the spiritual world with an essentially higher kind of consciousness than he has during his physical life on Earth.

When we are living here on Earth in our physical body, the earthly consciousness that is connected with the senses and nerves depends upon the whole organism. We feel ourselves as human beings in as much as within the boundary of our skin we have brain, lungs, heart, and the systems connected, with these organs. Of all this we say that it is *within* our being. On the other hand we feel ourselves connected with what is around us through our senses or through our breathing, or again through the taking of food. When we

1

are living between death and rebirth we cannot, however, speak in the same sense of what is 'within' us. For directly we pass through the gate of death, even directly we go to sleep, the conditions of our existence are such that the whole universe may be designated as our inner being.

Thus whereas here on Earth our constitution as human beings is revealed by our organs and their interaction inside our skin, during sleep unconsciously but between death and a new birth in full consciousness, our inner nature is revealed to us as if it were a world of stars. We feel ourselves related to the world of stars in such a way that of the Beings of the stars we say that they are our inner nature, just as here on Earth we say that the lung or heart belong to our inner physical nature. From the time of going to sleep until that of waking, we have a cosmic *life;* from death until a new birth we have a cosmic *consciousness.* That which here on Earth is our *outer* world, particularly when we gaze out into the cosmic expanse, becomes our *inner* being after death.

What, then, is our outer world in that spiritual existence? It is what is now our *inner* nature. We fashion what is then our outer world into a kind of spirit-seed from which our future physical body on Earth is to spring into existence. Together with the Beings of the Higher Hierarchies we elaborate this spirit-seed, and at a certain point of time in our life between death and a new birth, it is there as a spirit-entity, bearing within it the forces which then build up the physical body, just as the seed of the plant bears within it the forces which will eventually produce the plant. But whereas we picture the seed of the plant to be minute and the plant itself large in comparison, the spirit-seed of the human physical body is, so to speak, a universe of vast magnitude—although in the strict sense it is not quite accurate to speak of 'magnitude' in this connection.

I have also said that at a certain point this spirit-seed falls away from us. From a certain point of time onwards we feel: in association with other Beings of the Universe, with Beings of the Higher Hierarchies, we have brought the spirit-seed of our physical organism to a definite stage of development; now it falls away from us and descends into the physical forces of the Earth with which it is related and which come from the father and the mother. It unites with the human element in the stream of heredity and goes down to the Earth before we, as beings of spirit-and-soul, ourselves descend. Thus we still spend a certain period—although a short one— in the spiritual world when the nexus of forces of our physical organism has already gone down to the Earth and is shaping the embryo in the body of the mother.

It is during this period that we gather together from the cosmic ether its own forces and substances and so build up our etheric body to be added to our astral body and ego. Then, as a being of ego, astral body and etheric body, we ourselves come down to the Earth and unite with what the physical body—the seed of which was sent down earlier—has now become.

To anyone who observes this process closely, the relation of man to the Universe becomes very clear, above all if attention is directed to three manifestations of human nature to which reference has often been made here and at other places —I mean the three manifestations of human nature by virtue of which man becomes the being that he is on Earth.

When we are born we are quite different from the beings we afterwards become. It is on the Earth that we first learn to *walk*, to *speak*, and to *think*. The *will* that remains dim between birth and death, and *feeling* that remains half dim, are already present in a primitive form in the very tiny child. The life of feeling, although it is concerned entirely with the inner functions, is present in the very earliest years of child-hood. The life of will is also present, as is proved by the movements, however chaotic, made by the little child. The reason why the life of feeling and the life of will become different at a later stage of existence is that *thinking* grad-ually begins to permeate feeling and will, making them more mature. Nevertheless they are already present in the tiny child. Thinking, on the other hand, is developed by the child only on Earth, in association with other human beings and in a certain sense under their instruction. And it is the same with the faculties of walking and speaking, which in reality are acquired before the faculty of thinking.

Anyone who has a sufficiently deep feeling for what is truly human will realize, simply by observing how the child develops through walking, speaking, and thinking, what a tremendously important part is played by these three faculties in the earthly evolution of man. But man is not only an earthly being; he is a being who belongs not only to the Earth with its forces and substances, but equally to the spiritual world; he is involved in the activities proceeding between the several Beings of the Higher Hierarchies. It is, so to speak, only with a part of his being that man belongs to earthly existence; with the other part he belongs to a world that is not the material world perceptible to the senses. It is in that other world that he prepares his spirit-seed. Let it never be imagined that man's achievements in culture and civilization on the Earth, however complex and splendid they may be, are at all comparable with the greatness of what is achieved by him together with the Beings of the Higher Hierarchies in order to build this wonder-structure of the human physical organism. Nevertheless, what is thus fash-ioned—first of all in the spiritual world and, as I explained, sent down to the Earth *before* the man himself descends—

is differently constituted from the being who is afterwards present here on Earth between birth and death.

The spirit-seed of his physical body built up by man in the spiritual world is imbued with forces. Its whole structure which afterwards unites with the physical seed—or rather, which *becomes* the physical seed of the human being by taking substances from the parents—is endowed with all kinds of qualities and faculties. But there are three faculties for which the spirit-seed receives no forces at all in the spiritual world. These three faculties are: *thinking, speaking,* and *walking*— which are essentially activities of man on the Earth.

Let us take walking, and everything that is related to it. I might describe it as the process whereby man orientates himself within the sphere of his physical existence on Earth. When I move my arm or my hand, that too is related to the mechanism of walking, and when a tiny child begins to raise itself upright, that is an act of orientation. All this is connected with what we call the Earth's force of gravity, with the fact that everything physical on the Earth has *weight*. But we cannot say of the spirit-seed that is built up between death and a new birth that it has weight or heaviness.— Walking, then, is connected with the force of gravity. It is, in fact, an overcoming of gravity, an act through which we place ourselves into the field of gravity. That is what happens every time we lift a leg to take a step forward. But we do not acquire this faculty until we are already here on Earth; it is not present between death and a new birth although there is something that corresponds to it in that world. There too we have orientation but it is not orientation within the field of gravity, for in the spiritual world there is no force of gravity, no weight. Orientation in that world is of a purely spiritual character. Here on the Earth we lift our legs to walk, we place ourselves in the field of gravity. The cor-

5

responding process in the spiritual world is that of becoming related to some Being of the Higher Hierarchies, belonging, let us say, to the rank of Angel or Archangel. A man feels himself inwardly near in soul to the influence of a Being, say, of the Hierarchy of the Angels, or of the Exusiai, with whom he is then working. This is how he finds his orientation in the life between death and a new birth. Just as here on the Earth we have to deal with our weight, in yonder world we have to deal with what proceeds from the several Beings of the higher Hierarchies by way of forces of sympathy with our own human individuality.

The force of gravity has a single direction—towards the Earth; but what corresponds to the force of gravity in the spiritual world has *all* directions, for the spiritual Beings of the Hierarchies are not centralized, they are everywhere. The orientation is not geometrical like the orientation of gravity, towards the center of the Earth, but it goes in all directions. According to whether man has to build up his lung or perform some other work together with the Beings of the Hierarchies, he can say to himself: The Third Hierarchy is attracting me, or the First Hierarchy is attracting me. He feels himself placed into the whole world of the Hierarchies. He feels himself, as it were, drawn to all sides, not physically, as through the pull of gravity, but spiritually, or also, in some cases, repelled. This is what corresponds in the spiritual world to physical orientation within the sphere of gravity on the Earth.

Here, on the Earth, we learn to speak. This again belongs to our inherent nature, but within the spiritual world between death and a new birth we cannot speak; the physical organs needed for speech are not there. In the spiritual world between death and a new birth, we have, however, the following experience.—We feel ourselves in rhythmically alternat-

6

ing conditions; at one moment we have contracted, as it were, into our own being; our higher consciousness also contracts. Between death and a new birth there are times when we shut ourselves within ourselves, just as we do while we are asleep on Earth. But then we open ourselves again. Just as on the physical Earth we direct our eyes and other senses out towards the Universe, so in that other world we direct our spiritual organs of perception outwards to the Beings of the Hierarchies. We let our being stream out, as it were, into the far spaces, and then draw it together again.

It is a spiritual breathing process, but its course is such that if we were to describe in earthly words, in pictures derived from earthly life, what man says to himself there in the spiritual world, we should have to speak somewhat as follows: I, as a human being in the spiritual world, have this or that to do. I know this through the powers of perception I have in the spiritual world between death and a new birth. I feel myself to be this human being, this individuality. As I breathe out on Earth, so do I pour myself out in soul into the Universe and become one with the Cosmos. As I breathe in on Earth, so do I receive back into myself what I experienced while my being was poured out into the Cosmos.— This is constantly taking place between death and a new birth.

Let us think of a man feeling himself enclosed within his own being and then as though expanded into the cosmos. At one moment he is concentrated in himself and then has expanded into the Universe. When he draws into himself again it is just as when we breathe in the air from the physical spaces of the Universe.

Now when we have poured our being over the Cosmos and draw it in again, it begins—I cannot express it otherwise— it begins to tell us what it was that we embraced when our being was outspread as it were, in the cosmic expanse. When

7

we draw our being together again it begins to tell us what it is in reality, and we then say, between death and a new birth: The *Logos* in whom we first immersed ourselves—the *Logos* is speaking within us.

Here on the Earth we have the feeling that in our physical speech we shape the words when we exhale. Between death and a new birth we become aware that the words which are outspread in the Universe and reveal its essential nature, enter into us when our being is inbreathed and manifest themselves within us as the *Cosmic Word*. Here on Earth we speak as we breathe out; in the spiritual world we speak as we breathe in. And as we unite with our own being what the Logos—the Cosmic Word—says to us, the *Cosmic Thoughts* light up within our being. Here on Earth we make efforts through our nervous system to harbor earthly thoughts. In the spiritual world we draw into ourselves the Cosmic Thoughts out of the Cosmic Speech of the Logos when our being has been spread over the Universe.

Now try to form a vivid conception of the following. Suppose that you say to yourself between death and a new birth: I have this or that to do . . . all that you have experienced hitherto makes you aware that you have this or that task to perform. Then, with the intention of performing it, you spread your being into the Universe; but the process of expansion is actually one of orientation.

When you say to yourself here on Earth that you must buy some butter . . . that too signifies an intention. You set out for Basle to buy your butter there, and bring it home with you. Between death and a new birth you also have intentions—in connection, of course, with what has to be achieved in that other world. Then you expand your being; this is done with the intention of acquiring orientation—it may be that you are drawn to an Angel or perhaps to a Being of

8

Will, or to some other Being. Such a Being unites with your own expanded being. You breathe in; this Being communicates to you its participation in the Logos and the Cosmic Thoughts connected with this Being light up within you.

When the spirit-seed of man comes down to the Earth (as I have said, he himself remains a little while longer in the spiritual world), he is not organized for thinking or speaking in the earthly sense, nor for walking in the earthly sense, when gravity is involved; but he is organized for movement and for orientation among the Beings of the Higher Hierarchies. He is not organized for speaking but for enabling the Logos to resound within him. He is not organized for the shadowy thoughts of earthly life, but for the thoughts that become radiant in him, within the Cosmos.

Walking, speaking, and thinking here on the Earth have their correspondences in the spiritual world: in the *orientation among the Hierarchies,* in the *resounding of the Cosmic Word,* and in the inner *lighting up of the Cosmic Thoughts.*

Picture vividly to yourselves how man goes out after death into the wide space of the Cosmos. He passes through the planetary spheres around the Earth. I have spoken of these things in recent lectures here. He passes the Moon-sphere, the Venus-sphere, the Mercury-sphere, the Jupiter-sphere, the Saturn-sphere. Having passed right out into the Cosmos he will see the stars always from the other side. You must picture the Earth and the stars around it. From the Earth we look up to the stars; but when we are in the Cosmos we look from outside inwards. The forces that enable us here on Earth to see the stars, give us the physical image of the stars. The forces that enable us to see the stars from the other side, do not allow them to appear to us as they do here, but from that other world the stars appear to us as spiritual Beings.

And then, when we leave the planetary spheres—I am obliged to use earthly expressions—then, as conditions now are in world-evolution (the 'now' is, of course, a cosmic 'now' of lengthy duration), we realize with the understanding acquired through the higher consciousness belonging to our life between death and a new birth, what an infinite blessing it is for us that the forces of Saturn not only shine inwards into the planetary world of the Earth, but also outwards into the cosmic expanse. There, of course, they are something altogether different from the tiny, insignificant, bluish rays of Saturn that can be visible to us here on Earth. There they are spiritual rays, radiating out into the Universe—even ceasing to be spatial; they *radiate into a sphere beyond space.* They appear to us in such a way that between death and rebirth we look back in gratitude to the outermost planet of our earthly planetary system (for Uranus and Neptune are not actual Earth planets; they were added at a later stage). We are aware that this outermost planet not only shines down upon the Earth but out into the far spaces of the Cosmos. And to the spiritual rays which it radiates out into the Cosmos we owe the fact that we are now divested of earthly gravity, divested of the physical forces of speech, divested of the physical forces of thought. Saturn, as it radiates out into cosmic space is in very truth our greatest benefactor between death and a new birth. Regarded from a spiritual standpoint it constitutes, in this respect, the very antithesis of the Moon-forces.

The spiritual Moon-forces keep us on the Earth. The spiritual Saturn-forces enable us to live in the wide expanse of the Universe. Here, on Earth, the Moon-forces are of very special significance for us as human beings. I have explained that they play their part even in the everyday happening of waking from sleep. What the Moon-forces are for us here on Earth, the Saturn-forces that radiate into the Universe from the outermost sphere of our planetary system are for us between death and a new birth. You must not picture that from one side Saturn radiates towards the Earth and from another out into the Universe. It is not so. The physical Saturn appears like a hollow in this sphere of the cosmic Saturn which radiates, spiritually, into cosmic space. And from a certain point of time onwards after death, what thus radiates outwards hides everything earthly from us—hides it all with light.

Here on Earth, man is under the influence of the spiritual Moon-forces; between death and a new birth, he is under the influence of the Saturn-forces. And when he descends again to the Earth he draws himself away from the Saturn-forces and enters gradually into the sphere of the Moon-forces. What happens then?

As long as man is related to the sphere of the Saturn-forces—and Saturn is helped by Jupiter and Mars which have special functions to perform of which I shall speak on some future occasion—as long, therefore, as man is under the influence of Saturn, Jupiter and Mars, he is a being who does not strive to walk or speak or think in the earthly sense, but to find his orientation among spiritual Beings, to experience the Logos resounding within him, to have the Cosmic Thoughts lighting up within him. And with these inner aims and intentions the spirit-seed of the physical organism is, in very truth, dispatched to the Earth.

In effect, the human being who is descending from the spiritual worlds to the Earth has not the least inclination to be exposed to earthly gravity, to walk, or to bring the organs of speech into movement so that physical speech may resound, neither has he any inclination to think with a physical brain about physical things. He has none of these faculties. He only acquires them when, as a physical spirit-seed, he is sent down from the sphere of the Saturn-forces to the Earth, passes through the Sun-sphere and then enters the other planetary spheres—the spheres of Mercury, Venus and Moon. The Mercury, Venus, and Moon-spheres transform the cosmic predisposition for spiritual orientation, experience of the Logos and lighting up of Cosmic Thoughts inwardly, into the rudimental faculties of walking, speaking, and thinking. And the actual change is effected by the Sun, that is to say, the *spiritual* Sun.

Through the fact that man enters the sphere of the Moon—and the Moon-forces are helped by those of Venus and Mercury—through this, the heavenly predispositions for orientation, for experience of the Logos, and for Cosmic Thought, are transformed into the earthly faculties. Thus to a child here on Earth, as he begins to raise himself upright from the crawling position, we ought in truth to say: Before you were received into the spheres of Mercury, Venus and Moon, yonder in the heavenly spheres you were organized for spiritual orientation among the Hierarchies, for inner experience of the resounding Logos, and for inner illumination with Cosmic Thoughts. You have accomplished the metamorphosis from yonder heavenly faculties into earthly faculties in that you passed through the whole planetary sphere, and transformation of the Heavenly into the Earthly was wrought by the Sun.

But while this is happening, something else of tremendous significance takes place. Passing from the heavenly into the earthly realm, the human being experiences one side only of the etheric world. The etheric world extends through all the spheres of the planets and the stars. But the moment the heavenly faculties are transformed into the earthly, the human being loses the experience of the *Cosmic Morality*. Orientation among the Beings of the Higher Hierarchies is experienced not merely as a manifestation of natural laws but as *moral* orientation. Likewise the Logos speaks in the human being not in an a-moral way as do the phenomena of Nature—for although they do not speak in an anti-moral way, they speak 'a-morally.' The Logos speaks morality; so too the Cosmic Thoughts light up as bearers of morality.

Saturn, Jupiter and Mars—this must be said despite the horror it will cause to physicists—Saturn, Jupiter and Mars contain, as well as their other forces, forces of moral orientation. It is only when man transforms the heavenly faculties that have been characterized into walking, speaking, and thinking that he loses the moral elements. This is of immense importance. When here on Earth we speak of the ether—in which we live when we are approaching the Earth in order to be born—we ascribe to the ether all kinds of qualities. But that is only one side, one aspect, of the ether. The other aspect is that it is a substance working with a moral effect. It is permeated through and through with moral impulses. Just as it is permeated with light, so it is permeated with moral impulses. In the earthly ether these impulses are not present.

Yet man as an earthly being is not altogether bereft of the forces within which he lives between death and a new birth. Even if by some decree in the divine World-Order, man on the Earth had no inkling whatever that as well as having a physical nature he ought also to be a moral being, it might conceivably be that his earthly faculties of walking, speaking, and thinking would be dimly felt to correspond to a heavenly Orientation, a heavenly Logos, a heavenly illumination with Cosmic Thoughts. True, without some inner stimulus man knows very little on Earth of these heavenly correspondences of his earthly faculties; but for all that he has faint inklings of them. If there were no after-effects of the Heavenly here on Earth, every link binding man with the spiritual world would have been forgotten, leaving not a single trace. Even conscience would not stir.—I will take my start from something quite concrete, and although what I shall now say will seem strange to begin with, it is in exact accordance with facts established by spiritual research.

Think of the Earth with the air around it; farther outward is the cosmic ether, gradually passing over into the spiritual sphere. Here on the Earth we inhale and exhale the air. This is the rhythm of breathing. But out yonder we pour our being into the Cosmos, receiving into ourselves the Logos and the Cosmic Thoughts. There we let the World, the Universe, speak in us. This too takes place in rhythm—in a rhythm determined by the world of the stars. Out in the Cosmos there is also rhythm. As human beings on the Earth we have the rhythm of breathing, which is related in a definite way to the rhythm of blood-circulation: four pulse-beats to one breath. In yonder world, we breathe out and breathe in again spiritually; this is cosmic rhythm. As men on Earth our life depends upon the fact that we take a definite number of breaths a minute and have a definite number of pulse-beats a minute. Out in the Universe we live in a cosmic rhythm, in that we breathe in, as it were, the moral-ethereal world; we are then within ourselves. And when we breathe it out again we are united with the Beings of the Higher Hierarchies.

Just as here in our physical body inside our skin, regular movements are set going rhythmically, so out in the universe the course and the positions of the stars set the cosmic rhythm into which we pass between death and a new birth. We live in the air, and in the air unfold our breathing rhythm with its extraordinarily true regularity. If the rhythm is

14

irregular, this betokens illness for man. Out in the Universe
—although we have first to pass through intermediate cosmic
space—we experience the cosmic rhythm inasmuch as we
are then living in the cosmic ether, permeated as it is with the
moral element. Thus there are two different rhythms: human and cosmic. In truth they are both human rhythms, for
the cosmic rhythm is the human rhythm between death and
a new birth.

On the Earth, the Universe has, so to speak, the rhythm
proper to mankind; in yonder world it has the rhythm in
which we ourselves participate between death and rebirth.
What, then, lies between the two? The rhythm proper to
mankind gives us the faculty between birth and death to
speak human words, to master human language. Cosmic
rhythm enables us between death and a new birth to let the
Cosmic Word resound within us. The Earth endows us with
the gift of speech. The Universe, the spiritual Universe,
gives us the Logos. You will realize that conditions are
utterly different in the sphere where cosmic rhythm gives us
the Logos, from conditions here on the Earth, where we
articulate the human word in the air.

What, then, constitutes the boundary between the one
realm and the other? Looking out into the physical world we
have no perception of the cosmic rhythm. There is inner
law and order in each realm, so what is it that lies between
them? Between them—if I may put it so—is the boundary at
which the cosmic rhythm breaks in that it is coming too near
the Earth; between them is that which, in certain circumstances, may also bring the human breathing-rhythm into
disorder. Between them, in effect, are all the phenomena
pertaining to *meteorology*. If on the Earth there were no
blizzards, storms, wind, cloud formations, if the air did not
contain, in addition to oxygen and nitrogen for our breath-

ing, these meteorological phenomena which are always there, however clear the air may appear to be—then we should look out into the Universe and be aware of a different rhythm— actually the counterpart of our breathing rhythm, only transformed into infinite grandeur. Between the two spheres of the World-Order lie the chaotic phenomena of wind and weather, separating the cosmic rhythm and the human breathing rhythm from each other.

Man on the Earth is subject to gravity. He co-ordinates his gait, every movement of his hands with this force of gravity. Out in the Universe the forces are altogether different. Orientation there is in all directions; the lines of force run from Being to Being of the Hierarchies. What is between the two? As meteorological phenomena are between heavenly rhythm and human rhythm on Earth, what is between the cosmic force that is the opposite of gravity and earthly gravity?

Now just as meteorological phenomena lie between the two rhythms, so between the force of gravity and the opposite heavenly force of orientation there lie the *volcanic forces,* the forces which manifest in earthquakes. These are *irregular* forces.

(*Note by translator.* At this point in the lecture, Dr. Steiner referred to the report alleging that Easter Island, far out in the Pacific Ocean with its marvellous relics of ancient civilizations had been destroyed by a terrible earthquake. It will be remembered that the report was afterwards found to have been incorrect.)

When viewed from the standpoint of the Cosmos in the way I have described, the forces working in meteorological phenomena are intimately connected with our breathing proc-

16

esses. What takes place in the operations of volcanic forces is connected with the forces of gravity in such a way that it would really seem as though from time to time the super-sensible Powers were taking back fragments of the Earth by interfering with the laws of gravity and casting into chaos what the forces of gravity have gradually built up, in order to take it back again.

All earthly formations built up by the force of gravity are subject to these terrestrial phenomena. But whereas in the manifestations of weather the elements of air, warmth, and water are astir, in this case it is the solid and the watery elements that are involved. Here we have to do with forces that lead beyond the sphere of the regular laws of weight and gravity and which in course of time will do away with the Earth.

Now as well as the meteorological and volcanic manifestations there is a third kind of which I shall speak on another occasion. Ordinary science does not really know what to make of volcanic phenomena and often gives an explanation similar to the one I read just now in connection with the appalling earthquake which affected Easter Island. The author of an article on what was said to have happened was a geologist—therefore one possessed of expert knowledge in that particular domain. Having referred to what had happened, he added: When we reflect about the cause of these phenomena which recur from time to time and cause such destruction, we must include this recent earthquake in the category of tectonic tremors of the Earth.—What does this tell us? 'Tectonic tremors of the Earth' are tremors which cause an upheaval among portions of the Earth. So if we are to speak of the cause of such an upheaval, we must speak of the upheaval! Poverty comes from *pauvreté!*

It is indeed a fact that in order to see the connections be-

17

tween these things, we must approach the Spiritual. The moment we pass from the realm of ordinary natural law in some sphere—that of gravity, for example, or of rhythmic phenomena in the ether—the moment we pass from this into what is an apparent chaos (although through this chaos we are led into higher realms of the Cosmos) . . . in other words, if we are to understand volcanic and meteorological phenomena, we *must* turn towards the Spiritual.

Happenings in world-existence that seem to be purely fortuitous—for so we call them—are revealed in the spiritual realm in their lawful setting. It is through the working of the meteorological domain that we, as human beings between birth and death, are taken out of the sphere in which we live between death and a new birth. If instead of the many abstractions current at the present time we are to speak concretely, we may say: In the Heavens man lives in a World-Order that is hidden from him here on Earth through the fact that he is involved in the meteorological phenomena of the surrounding atmosphere. The meteorological domain is the dividing-wall between what man experiences on the Earth and what he experiences between death and a new birth.

In this way I want, if I can, to show you the realities of these things, not merely to talk round them.

II

Moral Qualities and the Life After Death.
Windows of the Earth.

Dornach, December 1, 1922

THE essential purpose of the lectures I have been giving here for some weeks past was to show how through his spiritual life man partakes in what we may call the world of the Stars, just as through his physical life on Earth he partakes in earthly existence, earthly happenings. In the light of the outlook acquired through Anthroposophy we distinguish in man the forces that lie in his physical body and in his etheric or formative-forces body, and those that lie in his Ego and his astral body. You know, of course, that these two sides of his being are separated whenever he sleeps. And now we will think for a short time of a man while he is asleep. On the one side the physical body and the etheric body lie there in a state of unconsciousness; but the Ego and the astral body are also without consciousness.

We may now ask: Are these two unconscious sides of human nature also related during sleep?—We know indeed that in the waking state, where the ordinary consciousness of modern man functions, the two sides are related through thinking, through feeling and through willing. We must therefore picture to ourselves that when the Ego and astral body plunge down, as it were, into the etheric body and the physical body, thinking, feeling, and willing arise from this union.

Now when man is asleep, thinking, feeling, and willing

cease. But when we consider his physical body we shall have to say: All the forces which, according to our human observation belong to Earth-existence are active in this physical body. This physical body can be weighed; put it on scales and it will prove to have a certain weight. We can investigate how material processes take their course within it—or at least we can imagine hypothetically that this is possible. We should find in it material processes that are a continuation of those processes to be found outside in Earth-existence; these continue within man's physical body in the process of nutrition. In his physical body we should also find what is achieved through the breathing process. It is only what proceeds from the head-organization of man, all that belongs to the system of senses and nerves, that is either dimmed or plunged in complete darkness during sleep.

If we then pass on to consider the etheric body which permeates the physical, it is by no means so easy to understand how this etheric body works during sleep. Anyone, however, who is already versed to a certain extent in what Spiritual Science has to say about man will realize without difficulty how through his etheric body the human being lives, even while asleep, amid all the conditions of the ether-world and all the etheric forces surrounding existence on Earth. So that we can say: Within the physical body of man while he is asleep, everything that belongs to Earth-existence is active. So too in the etheric body all that belongs to the ether-world enveloping and permeating the Earth is active.

But matters become more difficult when we turn our attention—naturally our soul's attention—to what is now (during sleep) outside the physical and etheric bodies, namely, to the Ego and astral body of man. We cannot possibly accept the idea that this has anything to do with the physical Earth, or with what surrounds and permeates the Earth as ether. As to what takes place during sleep, I indicated it to you in a more descriptive way in the lectures given here a short time ago, and I will outline it today from a different point of view. We can in reality only understand what goes on in the Ego and astral body of man when with the help of Spiritual Science we penetrate into what takes place on and around the Earth over and above the physical and etheric forces and activities.

To begin with, we turn our gaze upon the plant-world. Speaking in the general sense and leaving out of account evergreen trees and the like—we see the plant-world sprouting out of the Earth in spring. We see the plants becoming richer and richer in color, more luxuriant, and then in autumn fading away again. In a certain sense we see them disappear from the Earth when the Earth is covered with snow.

But that is only one aspect of the unfolding of the plant-world. Physical knowledge tells us that this unfolding of the plant-world in spring and its fading towards autumn is connected with the Sun, also that, for example, the green coloring of the plants can be produced only under the influence of sunlight. Physical knowledge, therefore, shows us what comes about in the realm of physical effects; but it does not show us that while all the budding, the blossoming and withering of the plants is going on, spiritual events are also taking place. In reality, just as in the physical human organism there is for example the circulation of the blood, just as etheric processes express themselves in the physical organism as vascular action and so forth, and just as this physical organism is permeated by the soul and spirit, so also the processes of sprouting, greening, blossoming and fading

21

of the plants which we regard as physical processes, are every-where permeated by workings of the cosmic world of soul and spirit.

Now when we look into the countenance of a man and his glance falls on us, when we see his expression, maybe the flushing of the face, then indeed the eyes of our soul are looking right through the physical to the soul and spirit. Indeed, it cannot be otherwise in our life among our fellow-men. In like manner we must accustom ourselves also to see spirit-and-soul in the physiognomy—if I may call it so—and changing coloring of the plant-world on our Earth.

If we are only willing to recognize the physical, we say that the Sun's warmth and light work upon the plants, form-ing in them the saps, the chlorophyll and so forth. But if we contemplate all this with spiritual insight, if we take the same attitude to this plant-physiognomy of the Earth as we are accustomed to take to the human physiognomy, then some-thing unveils itself to us that I should like to express with a particular word, because this word actually conveys the reality.

The Sun, of which we say, outwardly speaking, that it sends its light to the Earth, is not merely a radiant globe of gas but infinitely more than that. It sends its rays down to the Earth but whenever we look at the Sun it is the outer side of the rays that we see. The rays have, however, an inner side. If someone were able to look through the Sun's light, to regard the light only as an outer husk and look through to the soul of it, he would behold the Soul-Power, the Soul-Being of the Sun. With ordinary human consciousness we see the Sun as we should see a man who was made of papier-maché. An effigy in which there is nothing but the form, the lifeless form, is of course something different from the human being we actually see before us. In the case of the living human being, we see through this outer form and perceive soul-and-spirit. For ordinary consciousness the Sun is changed as it were into a papier-maché cast. We do not see through its outer husk that is woven of Light.

But if we were able to see through this, we should see the soul-and-spirit essence of the Sun. We can be conscious of its activity just as we are conscious of the physical papier-maché husk of the Sun. From the standpoint of physical knowledge we say: 'The Sun shines upon the Earth; it sparkles upon the stones, upon the soil. The light is thrown back and thereby we see everything that is mineral. The rays of the Sun penetrate into the plants, making them green, making them bud.'—All that is external. If we see the soul-and-spirit essence of the Sun, we cannot merely say: 'The sunlight sparkles on the minerals, is reflected, enabling us to see the minerals,' or, 'The light and heat of the Sun penetrate into the plants, making them verdant'—but we shall have to say, meaning now the countless spiritual Beings who people the Sun and who constitute its soul and spirit: 'The Sun dreams and its dreams envelop the Earth and fashion the plants.'

If you picture the surface of the Earth with the physical plants growing from it, coming to blossom, you have there the working of the physical rays of the Sun. But above it is the weaving life of the dream-world of the Sun—a world of pure Imaginations. And one can say: When the mantle of snow melts in the spring, the Sun regains its power, then the Sun-Imaginations weave anew around the Earth. These Imaginations of the Sun are Imaginative forces, playing in upon the world of plants. Now although it is true that this Imaginative world—this Imaginative atmosphere surrounding the Earth—is very specially active from spring until autumn in any given region of the Earth, nevertheless this dreamlike character of the Sun's activity is also present in a certain way during the time of winter. Only during winter the dreams are, as it were, dull and brooding, whereas in summer they are mobile, creative, formative. Now it is in this element in which the Sun-Imaginations unfold that the Ego and astral body of man live and weave when they are outside the physical and etheric bodies.

You will realize from what I have said that sleep in summer is actually quite a different matter from sleep in winter, although in the present state of evolution, man's life and consciousness are so dull and lacking in vitality that these things go unperceived. In earlier times men distinguished very definitely through their feelings between winter-sleep and summer-sleep, and they knew too what meaning winter-sleep and summer-sleep had for them. In those ancient times men knew that of summer-sleep they could say: During the summer the Earth is enveloped by picture-thoughts. And they expressed this by saying: The Upper Gods come down during the summer and hover around the Earth; during the winter the Lower Gods ascend out of the Earth and hover around it.—This Imaginative world, differently constituted in winter and in summer, was conceived as the weaving of the Upper and the Lower Gods. But in those olden times it was also known that man himself, with his Ego and his astral body, lives in this world of weaving Imaginations.

Now the very truths of which I have here spoken, show us, if we ponder them in the light of Spiritual Science, in what connection man stands, even during his earthly existence, with the extra-earthly Universe. You see, in summer—when it is summer in any region of the Earth—the human being during his sleep is always woven around by a sharply contoured world of Cosmic Imaginations. The result is that during the time of summer he is, so to speak, pressed near to the

24

Earth with his soul and spirit. During the time of winter it is different. During winter the contours, the meshes, of the Cosmic Imaginations widen out, as it were. During the summer we live with our Ego and astral body while we are asleep within very clearly defined Imaginations, within manifold figures and forms. During winter the figures around the Earth are wide-meshed and the consequence of this is that whenever autumn begins, that which lives in our Ego and astral body is borne far out into the Universe by night. During summer and its heat, that which lives in our Ego and astral body remains more, so to speak, in the psycho-spiritual atmosphere of the human world. During winter this same content is borne out into the far distances of the Universe. Indeed without speaking figuratively, since one is saying something that is quite real, one can say: that which man cultivates in himself, in his soul, and which through his Ego and astral body he can draw out from his physical and etheric bodies between the times of going to sleep and waking—that stores itself up during the summer and streams out during winter into the wide expanse of the Cosmos.

Now we cannot conceive that we men shut ourselves away, as it were, in earthly existence and that the wide Universe knows nothing of us. It is far from being so. True, at the time of Midsummer man can conceal himself from the Spirits of the Universe, and he may also succeed in harboring reprehensible feelings of evil. The dense net of Imaginations does not let these feelings through; they still remain. And at Christmastime the Gods look in upon the Earth and everything that lives in man's nature is revealed and goes forth with his Ego and astral being. Using a picture which truly represents the facts, we may say: In winter the windows of the Earth open and the Angels and Archangels behold what men actually are on the Earth.

We on Earth have gradually accustomed ourselves in modern civilization to express all that we allow to pass as knowledge in humdrum, dry, unpoetic phrases. The higher Beings are ever poets, therefore we never give a true impression of their nature if we describe it in barren physical words; we must resort to words such as I have just now used: at Christmastime the Earth's windows open and through these windows the Angels and Archangels behold what men's deeds have been the whole year through. The Beings of the higher Hierarchies are poets and artists even in their thinking. The logic we are generally at pains to apply is only an outcome of the Earth's gravity—by which I do not at all imply that it is not highly useful on Earth.

It is what lives in the minds and hearts of men as I have just pictured it, that is of essential interest to these higher Beings; the Angels who look in through the Christmas windows are not interested in the speculations of professors; they overlook them. Nor, to begin with, are they much concerned with a man's thoughts. It is what goes on in his feelings, in his heart, that in its cosmic aspect is connected with the Sun's yearly course. So it is not so much whether we are foolish or clever on Earth that comes before the gaze of the Divine-Spiritual Beings at the time of Christmas, but simply whether we are good or evil men, whether we feel for others or are egoists. That is what is communicated to the cosmic worlds through the course of the yearly seasons.

You may believe that our thoughts remain near the Earth, because I have said that the Angels and Archangels are not concerned with them when they look in through the Christmas windows. They are not concerned with our thoughts because, if I may use a rather prosaic figure of speech, they receive the richer coinage, the more valuable coinage that is minted by the soul-and-spirit of man. And this more valuable coinage is minted by the heart, the feelings, by what a man is worth because of what his heart and feeling contain. For the Cosmos, our thoughts are only the small change, the lesser coinage, and this lesser coinage is spied out by subordinate spiritual beings every night. Whether we are foolish or clever is spied out for the Cosmos every night—not indeed for the very far regions of the Cosmos but only for the regions around the Earth—spied out by beings who are closest to the Earth in its environment and therefore the most subordinate in rank. The daily revolution of the Sun takes place in order to impart to the Cosmos the worth of our thoughts. Thus far do our thoughts extend; they belong merely to the environment of the Earth. The yearly revolution of the Sun takes place in order to carry our heart-nature, our feeling-nature, farther out into the cosmic worlds.

Our will-nature cannot be carried in this way out into the Cosmos, for the cycle of the day is strictly regulated. It runs its course in twenty-four hours. The yearly course of the Sun is strictly regulated too. We perceive the regularity of the daily cycle in the strictly logical sequences of our thoughts. The regularity of the yearly cycle—we perceive the after-effect of this in our heart and soul, in that there are certain feelings which say to one thing that a man does: it is good, and to another: it is bad.

But there is a third faculty in man, namely, the *will*. True, the will is bound up with feeling, and feeling cannot but say that certain actions are morally good, and others morally not good. But the will can do what is morally good and also what is morally not good. Here, then, there is no strict regularity. The relation of our will to our nature as human beings is not strictly regulated in the sense that thinking and feeling are regulated. We cannot call a bad action good, or a good action bad, nor can we call a logical thought illogical, an illogical thought logical. This is due to the fact that our thoughts stand under the influence of the daily revolution of the Sun, our feelings under the influence of its yearly revolution. The will, however, is left in the hands of humanity itself on Earth. And now a man might say: 'The most that happens to me is that if I think illogically, my illogical thoughts are carried out every night into the Cosmos and do mischief there—but what does that matter to me? I am not here to bring order into the Cosmos.' —Here on Earth, where his life is lived in illusion, a man might in certain circumstances speak like this, but between death and a new birth he would never do so. For between death and a new birth he himself is in the worlds in which he may have caused mischief through his foolish thoughts; and he must live through all the harm that he has done. So, too, between death and a new birth, he is in those worlds into which his feelings have flowed. But here again he might say on Earth: 'What lives in my feelings evaporates into the Cosmos; but I leave it to the Gods to deal with any harm that may have been caused there through me. My will, however, is not bound on Earth by any regulation.'—

The materialist who considers that man's life is limited to the time between birth and death, can never conceive that his will has any cosmic significance; neither can he conceive that human thoughts or feelings have any meaning for the Cosmos. But even one who knows quite well that thoughts have a cosmic significance as the result of the daily revolution of the Sun, and feelings through the yearly revolution— even he, when he sees what is accomplished on the Earth by the good or evil will-impulses of man, must turn away from the Cosmos and to human nature itself in order to see how what works in man's will goes out into the Cosmos. *For what works in man's will must be borne out into the Cosmos*

28

by man himself, and he bears it out when he passes through the gate of death. Therefore it is not through the daily or the yearly cycles but through the gate of death that man carries forth the good or the evil he has brought about here on Earth through his will.

It is a strange relationship that man has to the Cosmos in his life of soul. We say of our thoughts: 'We have thoughts but they are not subject to our arbitrary will; we must conform to the laws of the Universe when we think, otherwise we shall come into conflict with everything that goes on in the world.'—If a little child is standing in front of me, and I think: That is an old man—I may flatter myself that I have determined the thought, but I am certainly out of touch with the world. Thus in respect of our thoughts we are by no means independent, so little independent that our thoughts are carried out into the Cosmos by the daily cycle of the Sun. Nor are we independent in our life of feelings, for they are carried out through the yearly cycle of the Sun. Thus even during earthly life, that which lives in our head through our thoughts and, through our feelings in our breast, does not live only within us but also partakes in a cosmic existence. That alone which lives in our will we keep with us until our death. Then, when we have laid aside the body, when we have no longer anything to do with earthly forces, we bear it forth with us through the gate of death.

Man passes through the gate of death laden with what has come out of his acts of will. Just as here on Earth he has around him all that lives in minerals, plants, animals and in physical humanity, all that lives in clouds, streams, mountains, stars, in so far as they are externally visible through the light—just as he has all this around him during his existence between birth and death, so he has a world around him when he has laid aside the physical and etheric bodies

29

and has passed through the gate of death. In truth he has around him the very world into which his thoughts have entered every night, into which his feelings have entered with the fulfilment of every yearly cycle . . . "That thou hast thought; that thou hast felt." . . . It now seems to him as though the Beings of the Hierarchies were bearing his thoughts and his feelings towards him. They have perceived it all, as I have indicated. His mental life and his feeling-life now stream towards him.

In earthly existence the Sun gives light from morning to evening; it goes down and night sets in. When we have passed through the gate of death, our wisdom rays out towards us as day; through our accumulated acts of folly, the spiritual lights grow dark and dim around us and it becomes night. Here on Earth we have day and night; when we have passed through the gate of death, we have as day and night the results of our wisdom and our foolishness. And what man experiences here on this Earth as spring, summer, autumn and winter in the yearly cycle, as changing temperatures and other sentient experiences, of all this he becomes aware—when he has passed through the gate of death—also as a kind of cycle, although of much longer duration. He experiences the warmth-giving, life-giving quality (life-giving, that is to say, for his spiritual Self) of his good feelings, of his sympathy with goodness; he experiences as icy cold his sympathy with evil, with the immoral. Just as here on Earth we live through the heat of summer and the cold of winter, so do we live after death warmed by our good feelings, chilled by our evil feelings; and we bear the effects of our will through these spiritual years and days. After death we are the product of our moral nature on Earth. And we have an environment that is permeated by our follies and our wisdom, by our sympathies and antipathies for the good.

So that we can say: Just as here on Earth we have the summer air around us giving warmth and life, and as we have the cold and frosty winter air around us, so, after death, we are surrounded by an atmosphere of soul-and-spirit that is warm and life-giving in so far as it is produced through our good feelings, and chilling in so far as it is produced through our evil feelings. Here on Earth, in certain regions at least, the summer and winter temperatures are the same for all of us. In the time after death, each human being has *his own* atmosphere, engendered by himself. And the most moving experiences after death are connected with the fact that one man lives in icy cold and the other, close beside him, in life-giving warmth.

Such are the experiences that may be undergone after death. And as I described in my book *Theosophy,* one of the main experiences passed through in the soul-world, is that those human beings who have harbored evil feelings here on Earth, must undergo their hard experiences in the sight of those who developed and harbored good feelings.

It can indeed be said: All that remains concealed to begin with in the inner being of man, discloses itself when he has passed through the gate of death. Sleep too acquires a cosmic significance, likewise our life during wintertime. We sleep every night in order that we may prepare for ourselves the light in which we must live after death. We go through our winter experiences in order to prepare the soul-spiritual warmth into which we enter after death. And into this atmosphere of the spiritual world which we have ourselves prepared we bear the effects of our deeds.

Here on Earth we live, through our physical body, as beings subject to earthly gravity. Through our breathing we live in the surrounding air, and far away we see the stars. When we have passed through the gate of death we are in the world of spirit-and-soul, far removed from the Earth; we are beyond the stars, we see the stars from the other side, look back to the world of stars. Our very being lives in the cosmic thoughts and cosmic forces. We look back upon the stars, no longer seeing them shine, but seeing instead the Hierarchies, the Spiritual Beings who have merely their reflection in the stars.

Thus man on Earth can gain more and more knowledge of what the nature of his life will be when he passes through the gate of death. There are people who say: 'Why do I need to know all this? I shall surely see it all after death!'— That attitude is just as if a man were to doubt the value of eyesight. For as the Earth's evolution takes its course, man enters more and more into a life in which he must acquire the power to partake in these after-death experiences by grasping them, to begin with in thought, here on the Earth. To shut out knowledge of the spiritual worlds while we are on the Earth is to blind ourselves in soul and spirit after death. A man will enter the spiritual world as a cripple when he passes through the gate of death, if here, in this world, he disdains to learn about the world of spirit, for humanity is evolving towards freedom—towards free spiritual activity. This fact should become clearer and clearer to mankind and should make men realize the urgent necessity of gaining knowledge about the spiritual world.

III

Man's Relation to the World of the Stars.

Dornach, December 3, 1922

IN the course of our present studies I should like it to become increasingly clear that man does not belong to the Earth alone, to Earth-existence alone, but also to the Cosmos, to the world of Stars. Much of what there is to say in this connection I have, as you know, already said. I want now to begin with a brief remark in order that misunderstandings may be avoided.

Anyone who speaks of man's connection with the world of the Stars is probably always liable to be accused of leanings towards the superficial form of Astrology that is so widely pursued nowadays. But if what is said on this subject is rightly understood, the immense difference will at once be apparent between what is meant here and the amateurish interpretations of ancient astrological traditions that are so common today.

When we say that man, between birth and death, is a being connected with the Earth and earthly happenings, what do we mean by this? We mean that man owes his existence between birth and death to the fact that, in the first place, he takes the substances of the Earth into his metabolic system as nourishment and digests them; further, that through his breathing, and through the inner processes connected with his breathing, he is related in still another way to the Earth—that is to say, to the atmosphere surrounding the

the Earth. We also say that man perceives the outer things of the Earth by means of his senses, perceives indeed reflections of what is extra-terrestrial—reflections which are, however, of a much more earthly character than is generally supposed. So that in general one can say: Man partakes of earthly existence through his senses, through his rhythmic system, and through his metabolic system, and has within him the continuation of the processes set in operation through this Earth-existence itself.

But equally there takes place in man a continuation of cosmic, extra-terrestrial processes. Only it must not be supposed, when it is said that an influence from the Moon, or Venus, or Mars, is exercised upon man, that this is to be understood merely as if rays of light are sent down from Mars or Venus or the Moon, and permeate him. When, for instance, it is said that man is subject to the influence of the Moon, this must be taken as an analogy of what is meant by saying that man is subject to the influences of the substances of the Earth. When someone passes an apple-tree, let us say, picks an apple and eats it, it can be said that the apple-tree has an influence on him; but we should not construe this so literally as to say that the apple-tree had sent its rays towards him. Or, if you like, when a man passes a meadow where there is an ox, and a week afterwards eats its flesh, we shall not at once form the idea that the ox has exercised an influence upon him. Neither must we picture so literally what is said about the influence upon man of the world of the Stars. The relation of the world of the Stars to man and of man to the world of the Stars is for all that just as much a reality as the relation of the man to the ox he passes in the meadow and the flesh of which he afterwards eats.

Today I have to speak of certain connections which exist between man and the worlds both of Earth-existence and of

34

extra-earthly existence. If we again turn our attention to how man lives in the alternating conditions of waking and sleeping, we must first be clear that it is in the waking state that his reciprocal relationship to earthly substances and earthly forces is actually established. During waking life he perceives through his senses; during sleep he does not. Moreover he eats and drinks only when awake—though possibly some people would like to do so in sleep as well! The breathing process and the process that is connected with the breathing, i.e. the circulation of the blood, as well as the other rhythmic processes—these alone continue in man both in the waking and sleeping states. But they differ in the two states. I will speak later of the difference there is between breathing during waking life and breathing during sleep. To begin with we will confine ourselves to the fact that man is related to the outer world during the waking state through his senses and through his metabolism. We will consider this at first in connection only with things that are common knowledge.

Let us then start from the fact that during his waking state man takes foodstuffs into himself from the outside world, inner activity being promoted by the process of digestion. But it must not be forgotten that while, in the waking state, after the food has been taken, inner physical and etheric activity proceeds under the influence of the intaken foodstuffs, this physical and etheric organism of man is permeated by his Ego-organization and astral body.

It is also the case that during the waking state, man's Ego and astral 'being' take command of what goes on in the physical and etheric bodies in connection with the process of nourishment. But what thus takes place under the influence of the Ego and astral being does not continue during sleep. During sleep the physical and etheric bodies of man

35

are worked upon by forces that issue, not from the Earth but from the cosmic environment of the Earth—from the world of the Stars.

It might be said—and not in a figurative sense for it has real meaning—that by day man eats the substances of the Earth and by night takes into himself what the Stars and their activities give him. In a certain sense, therefore, man is bound up with the Earth while he is awake and removed from the Earth while he is asleep; heavenly processes take their course in his physical and etheric bodies during sleep.

Materialistic science thinks that when a man is asleep, the substances he has consumed simply activate their own forces in him, whereas in reality, whatever substances a man takes into himself are worked upon during his sleep by the cosmic forces in the environment of the Earth. Suppose, for instance, we consume white of egg—albumen. This albumen is only fettered to the Earth through the fact that during the waking state we are permeated by our soul and spirit—our astral body and Ego. During sleep this albumen is worked upon by the whole planetary system from Moon to Saturn, and by the world of the fixed Stars. And a chemist who wished to study the inner processes taking place in man during sleep would have not only to be versed in earthly chemistry but also in a spiritual chemistry, for the processes then are different from those that take their course during waking life.

The Ego and astral being of man are, as you know, separated from the physical and etheric bodies during sleep and are not directly related with the world of the Stars; but they *are* directly related with the Beings of whom the Sun, Moon and Stars are the physical mirror-images—namely, with the Beings of the Hierarchies. Man asleep is a duality; his Ego and astral body—I could equally well say, his spirit

36

and soul—become subject to the spiritual Beings of the higher kingdoms of the Universe. His bodies, the physical and etheric bodies, are subject to the physical reflections, the cosmic-physical mirror-images of these higher Beings.

Aware of himself as an earthly being, man has become more and more a materialistic philistine under the influence of intellectualism. Almost as aptly as the modern age is called the epoch of intellectual and scientific progress, it could be called the epoch of materialistic philistinism. For man is not conscious that he is dependent on anything else than sense-impressions coming from the Earth, the rhythmic processes set going in him by earthly processes, the metabolic processes also occasioned in him by earthly conditions. Hence he does not know his real place in the Universe. The factors in operation here are of tremendous complexity. As soon as the veil that is spread before man in order that he may see only the sense-world and not the spiritual world behind it, is drawn aside, life becomes extraordinarily complex.

It is found to begin with that man is influenced not only by those Beings and their physical reflections, the Stars, which can be directly observed, but that within earthly existence itself, supersensible Beings akin to those of the world of Stars have so to speak set up their abode in the earthly realm.

You know that the people of the Old Testament worshipped Jehovah—who was an actual Being, connected with what manifests in the physical world as Moon. It is of course more or less a figure of speech to say that the Jehovah-Being has his dwelling in the Moon, but at the same time there is reality in the expression. Everything pertaining to this Jehovah-Being is connected with the Moon.

Now there are Beings who 'scorned'—if I may so express

it—to make the journey to the Moon with the Jehovah-beings when the Moon separated from the Earth, and who remained in the earthly realm. So that in a way we can divine the existence of the true Jehovah-beings when we look at the Moon. We can say: that is the outer physical image of everything that participates in a regular way in the World Order in connection with the Being known as Jehovah. But when we learn to know what takes place inside the surface of the Earth—whether in the solid or the watery states—we find beings there who have disdained to make their home on the Moon, and have in an irregular way made the Earth their dwelling-place.

Now the Moon-beings, as I will call them, have helpers. These helpers belong to Mercury and Venus, just as the Moon-beings belong to the Moon. The Venus-beings, the Mercury-beings and the Moon-beings form a kind of trinity. The so-called regular beings of this kind in the Universe belong to these Stars. But both in the solid and the watery constituents of the Earth, we find beings belonging, it is true, to the same category, but—one might say—to a different epoch of time. They are beings who did not share in the Earth's cosmic evolution.

These beings have an influence upon sleeping man just as the regular cosmic beings have; but their influence is pernicious. I must characterize it by saying: when a man goes to sleep, then in the condition between falling asleep and waking, these irregular Moon, Venus and Mercury-beings approach him and set about persuading him that evil is good and good evil. All this takes place in man's unconscious condition, between going to sleep and waking.

It is a shattering experience connected with initiation that beyond the threshold of ordinary consciousness things by no means without danger to humanity are encountered.

38

People holding the materialistic view of life have no idea to what man is exposed between going to sleep and waking. He is actually exposed to these beings who persuade him in his sleeping state that good is evil, and evil good. The moral order on Earth is bound up with the human etheric body, and when man sleeps, he leaves his moral achievements behind him on the bed. He does not pass over into the state of sleep armed with his moral qualities.

Natural Science today is everywhere touching the fringe of things which need to be explained by Spiritual Science. You may recently have seen in the newspapers some interesting and thoroughly well-founded statistics. It was stated that criminals in the prisons have been found to have the soundest sleep of all. Really hardened criminals are never tormented during their sleep by bad dreams or the like. This only happens when they dip down again into their etheric bodies, for it is there that the moral qualities lie. It can much more easily happen to one who is striving to be moral, that through the constitution of his etheric body, he carries over something into his astral body and is then tormented by dreams as the result of comparatively trifling moral lapses. But generally speaking it is a fact that man does not carry over at all, or only to a very slight extent, the moral constitution he acquires during earthly existence but is exposed during sleep to the beings just referred to.

These beings are identical with those I have always designated as Ahrimanic. They set themselves the task of keeping man on the Earth by every possible means. You know from the book *Occult Science* that the Earth will one day pass over into the Jupiter condition. That is what these beings want to prevent. They want to prevent man from developing in a regular way together with the Earth and then passing over into the Jupiter condition in a normal way. They want to preserve the Earth *as Earth* and mankind for the Earth. Hence these beings work unceasingly and with great intensity to achieve the following.—You must remember that these are things that take place behind the scenes of existence —real processes that have been going on ever since there has been a human race on the Earth.—Man passes into the state of sleep in his Ego-being and astral-being. These Moon, Venus and Mercury-beings who are living unlawfully on the Earth, now endeavor to give man an etheric body composed of the Earth's ether whenever he is asleep. They hardly ever succeed. In rare cases of which I will speak at some later time, they have succeeded; but this hardly ever happens. Still they do not give up the attempt for over and over again it seems to them that their efforts might succeed, that they might surround, permeate a man while he is asleep and has left his etheric body behind, with another etheric body built up from the Earth's ether. That is what these beings desire.

If an Ahrimanic being of this category were actually to succeed in bringing a complete etheric body stage by stage into a man every time he slept, such a man would be able after death, when living in his etheric body, to maintain himself in that body. Otherwise, as you know, the etheric body dissolves in a few days. But a man to whom the above had happened would be able to continue existing in his etheric body and after a time there would arise a race of etheric humanity. That is what is desired from this side of the spiritual world, and then it would be possible by such means to preserve the Earth.

Within the solid and the fluid components of the Earth there are in very truth a host of such beings. Their desire is to make mankind into pure phantoms, etheric phantoms, until the end of the Earth's evolution, so that the normal goal of Earth-evolution could not be attained. And in the night-time these beings by no means lose courage; over and over again they believe that their efforts may succeed.

Now man today has quite a passably good intellect which has developed considerably at the present time when philistinism is on the increase. Man can certainly pride himself upon possessing intellect. But this intellect is not even remotely on a par with the intellect of those higher beings who desire to achieve what I am now describing to you. Let nobody say: 'These beings must be fearfully stupid.' They are certainly not stupid. Seeing that they work only upon human beings in sleep, there is nothing to deter them from believing that they might succeed before the end of Earth-evolution in preventing a large portion of the human race from reaching their future destinations—destinations bound up with the Jupiter embodiment of the Earth.

But one who is able to see behind the scenes of physical existence can perceive that these beings do sometimes lose courage, are disappointed. And the disappointments they experience are not experienced in the night, but by day. One sees, for instance, how these Ahrimanic beings suffer disappointments if one comes across them in hospitals.

Now of course the illnesses that befall men have one aspect that calls upon us in all circumstances to do everything we possibly can to heal them. But on the other side we must ask: how do the illnesses suffered by men arise out of the dark sources of natural existence?

Those illnesses which are not the result of external influences but arise out of the inner constitution of man, are connected with the fact that when the Ahrimanic beings have almost succeeded in making a man assume an etheric body that is not his normal one, then, instead of bringing the lawful working of the etheric forces into his physical

41

body and into his own accustomed etheric body on waking, such a man bears into himself causes of illness. Through these causes of illness the true Venus, Mercury and Moon-beings protect themselves against the harmful influences of the irregular beings. Indeed if a man did not at some time or another get this or that illness, he would be liable to the danger of which I have just spoken. In any illness his body breaks down, collapses, in order that there can be 'sweated out,' if I may use the expression, whatever irregular etheric processes he has taken into himself through the Ahrimanic influences.

And a further reaction called forth in order to prevent man from falling a victim to this Ahrimanic influence, is the *possibility of error*. And a third thing is *egoism*. Man is not fundamentally intended to be ill, to fall a prey to error, or to be egoistic to an exaggerated degree. Egoism as such is again a means of holding man to the evolution proper to the Earth instead of being torn out of it by the Ahrimanic beings. This, then, is one order of beings which can be discovered behind the scenes of ordinary sense-existence.

One can form an idea of another order of beings by knowing that not only Moon, Mercury, and Venus have an influence upon man but that an influence is also exercised from beyond the Sun—from Mars, Jupiter, and Saturn.

You know from the lectures I gave in the so-called 'French Course' * that the Moon is the physical reflection of those beings who bring man into the physical world. Saturn is the physical reflection of those beings who bear him again out of the physical world. The Moon draws man down to

* Printed under the title: *Philosophy, Cosmology and Religion.* An abbreviated version of ten lectures given by Dr. Steiner in Dornach, 6th-15th September, 1922.

the Earth; Saturn draws him again into the Universe and then into the spiritual world.

Just as the Jehovah-Moon-God has Venus and Mercury-beings as helpers, so Saturn has Jupiter and Mars-beings as helpers in bearing man into the Cosmos and into the spiritual worlds. These influences and the influences connected with the Moon-beings work upon man in exactly the opposite way.

The influences of Moon, Venus, and Mercury upon us are predominant until our 17th or 18th years. Then later on, when we have passed our 20th or 21st year, an influence from Mars, Jupiter and Saturn becomes particularly active; only in later years does this come to the point of leading us out of earthly existence into the spiritual world. The inner constitution of man is, in fact, dependent upon this transition, as one might say, from the inner planets to the outer planets. Until our 17th or 18th years, we are dependent, for instance, upon the major blood-circulation which affects the whole body. Later in life we are dependent upon the minor blood-circulation—but these are matters which must be left for future lectures. At the moment we must pay attention to the fact that just as the irregular beings of Moon, Venus, and Mercury have their habitations in the solid and fluidic components of the Earth, so the irregular beings of Mars, Jupiter, and Saturn have the conditions for their existence —or, to speak pictorially, their habitations—in the warmth and in the air surrounding the Earth.

These beings have a great influence upon man during his sleeping state. But their influence works in exactly the opposite direction. The aim of *these* beings is to make man into a *moral automaton*—if I may so express it—into a moral automaton of such a nature that in his waking state he would not listen to his own instincts, his desires, or the voice of his blood, but would spurn all this and hearken only to the inspiration of these irregular Mars-, Jupiter-, and Saturn-beings. He would then become a moral automaton, without any prospect of a future state of freedom. That, then, is what these beings desire; and their influence too is strong, exceedingly strong. It is they who every night want to induce man to take the influence of the world of Stars into himself and never again the influence of the Earth. They would fain carry man right away from earthly existence. They desire—and have desired this ever since the human race first arose on the Earth—that man shall spurn the Earth, that he shall not awaken to freedom on the Earth—where alone this is possible. They desire that he shall remain a moral automaton as he was in the preceding metamorphosis of the Earth, in the Old Moon.

And in the middle, between these two hosts, of which the one sets its camp in the element of warmth and that of air, and the other in the elements of earth and of water—between these two opposing cosmic hosts stands Man. Life in his physical body conceals from him the fact that a fierce battle is waged in the Cosmos for possession of his being.

Today man must consciously find his way to such knowledge for it concerns him deeply and essentially. His very existence as a human being is constituted by the fact that forces are everywhere active around him, forces from the spiritual world. It is important for man today to have knowledge of his real position in the Universe.

A time will come when people will be far more justified in holding a poor opinion of our dark, materialistic knowledge compared with what will be known in the future about the spiritual reality behind the physical, than we are justified in saying that the scientific knowledge possessed by the Greeks was puerile, that they were mere children, whereas we have made splendid progress! In philistinism we certainly have made splendid progress and we shall have much more right to criticise when we can speak with full knowledge of this battle that is waging on the Earth for possession of man's being.

There are signs that a knowledge of these things must begin to spread in our time. It is certainly true that what I have told you today about the battle of the Ahrimanic and Luciferic beings in the Cosmos for the being of man is still hidden from the majority of people in the dark recesses of their inner nature. But these battles are now beginning to send their waves into that realm of existence of which men are clearly conscious. And today, if we are not to lead a sleepy existence in our civilization, we must know how to recognize the first waves that beat in upon us from those regions of the spiritual world which I have just characterized.

These two hosts—the Luciferic in the warmth and airy element of the Earth, the Ahrimanic in the solid and watery —these two hosts send their waves into our cultural life today. The Luciferic hosts are making their influence felt above all in outworn theology. In our cultural life, as an outflow of this Luciferic power, we encounter statements endeavoring to make Christ into a myth. The Christ descended to the Earth through the Mystery of Golgotha as a real Being, and that is naturally a truth that cuts right across the intentions of the beings who would like to make man into a moral automaton, without freedom. Therefore: Do away with the reality of Christ. Christ is a myth! You can discover in the literature of the 19th century, how clever and ingenious were the hypotheses of theologians like David Frederic Strauss, Kalthoff and those who merely echoed them, or better said, apish babblers like Arthur

Drews! Everywhere the view is advanced that Christ is a mythological figure, a mere picture which has impressed itself upon man's imagination.—There will be many more attacks from these hosts—but this is the first.

The first waves coming from the Ahrimanic host in the solid and watery elements of the Earth press home the opposite view. In this case, Christ is denied and validity allowed only to the 'simple man of Nazareth,' to Jesus as the physical personality. Here again is a tit-bit presented by theology!

Making Christ into a myth—a purely Luciferic activity. Making the One who went through the Mystery of Golgotha into a mere man—even if endowed with every possible quality—a purely Ahrimanic activity. This, however, does not succeed at all easily, for the many testimonies and traditions have to be eliminated before producing this 'simple man of Nazareth.' Nevertheless this other tit-bit of theology is evidence of the onrush of the Ahrimanic breakers into human culture.

If these things are to be rightly assessed we must be able also to detect them behind the scenes of our ordinary existence on Earth. Otherwise, if men are not willing to turn their attention to what can be said today out of the spiritual world, they will become less and less able to judge such phenomena correctly, and these phenomena will then take effect in the subconsciousness. It will become increasingly dangerous for men to surrender to the subconscious. Clear, thoughtful observation of what actually exists—a feeling for reality—that is the growing need of humanity.

Perhaps we can trace most definitely where this clear thoughtfulness, this sense of reality, must be applied, when we perceive the increase of such extraordinary phenomena as the theology which on the one hand denies Christ, and on the other hand makes Christ a myth. Such phenomena will become more and more prevalent, and if they are not to lead to corruption, humanity must acquire a clear, unswerving perception of the spiritual influences that are exercised upon the physical world, and particularly upon man himself.

I told you once before of the two men who found a piece of iron bent into a certain shape. The one said: "A good horse-shoe! I will shoe my horse with it." The other said: "Not at all. It is a magnet and can be used for quite different purposes than shoeing a horse!" "I see nothing like a magnet about it," said the other man. "You are crazy to say that there are invisible magnetic forces in it. It's a horse-shoe —that's its use!"

This is rather like the people today who are not willing to receive the knowledge that comes from the spiritual world. They want to "shoe horses" with everything in the world— if I may so express myself—because they will not acknowledge the reality of the supersensible forces. They want to shoe horses—not to make anything in which the magnetic forces are put to use. There was once a time—nor does it lie very far behind us—when a piece of iron so shaped would have been used for the shoeing of horses. But today this is no longer possible.

A time will come when in ordinary social life too, men will need what can be communicated from the spiritual world. Of this we must be mindful, and then Anthroposophy will penetrate not only into the intellect—that is of less importance—but above all into the *will*—and that is of great importance. Upon this we will ponder more and more deeply.

IV

Rhythms of Earthly and Spiritual Life.
Love, Memory, the Moral Life.

Dornach, December 15, 1922

LET us recall what I have been telling you about man's experiences between death and a new birth. The various descriptions have enabled us to realize that this life—above all in its main period, about the middle of the time between death and rebirth—is such that man lives in communion with the Beings referred to in the book *Occult Science* as the Beings of the Higher Hierarchies. This life of man in communion with those higher Beings is comparable with the life he has here, when in the physical body, in communion with the beings of the three kingdoms of Nature. Basically speaking, everything in his earthly environment belongs to one of the three kingdoms of Nature—to the mineral or the plant or the animal kingdom, or indeed the physical human kingdom, which in this particular connection can be taken as belonging to the animal kingdom.

Man has his senses, and through his sense-impressions he lives in communion with the beings of the three kingdoms of Nature. What unfolds in his life of feeling between birth and death, in so far as it is the outcome of experiences arising from his environment, is also related to these three kingdoms of Nature. The same applies to what comes from the will, namely, human action. Thus between birth and death man is interwoven with what his senses convey to him from the three kingdoms of Nature.

48

In like manner between death and a new birth, in the time indicated above, man lives within the higher realms, among the Beings of the Higher Hierarchies. This life together with the Beings of the Hierarchies is, in reality, all action, perpetual activity. We have heard how the spirit-seed of the physical body is produced in cooperation with these higher Beings. Here on Earth, when we perceive or connect ourselves with the entities belonging to the three kingdoms of Nature, we feel outside them. But there is a condition between death and a new birth when we find ourselves wholly within the Beings of the Higher Hierarchies; we are entirely given up to them. That is one of the conditions in which we then live.—Let us picture it clearly.—Here on the Earth, when, for example, we pick a flower, the fact is correctly described by saying, 'I pick the flower.' But if this way of speaking were applied to our life together with the Beings of the Higher Hierarchies, the facts would not then be correctly expressed. When we do something in connection with these Beings, we must say: *the other Being acts in us.* Thus we are in a condition which compels us all the time not to call the activity—in which of course we ourselves partake —our own activity, but the activity of the Beings of the Hierarchies in us. We have in very truth a cosmic consciousness. Just as here we feel heart, lungs and so on, to be within us, so do we then feel the world to be within us, but it is the world of the Beings of the Higher Hierarchies. Everything that takes place is the outcome of an activity in which we, too, are involved; but to describe the facts correctly we should have to say: such and such a Being of the Higher Hierarchies is acting in us.

Now the condition thus described is only one of the conditions obtaining between death and a new birth. We could not be men in the true sense if we lived in this one condition

49

only. In the spiritual world between death and rebirth we should no more be able to bear this condition only, than here on Earth we could bear inbreathing without exhaling. The condition I have just described must alternate with another, which consists in our obliterating through our cosmic consciousness all thinking and feeling about the Beings of the Higher Hierarchies, obliterating too all will that works in this way in us from the Beings of the Hierarchies.

Thus we may say that there are times during the life between death and a new birth when we find ourselves filled through and through with the Beings of the Higher Hierarchies and their radiance. We feel them within ourselves. But there is another condition, in which we have first suppressed and then obliterated altogether, this consciousness of the Higher Beings manifesting in us. Then—to use earthly terms—we are 'out of our body'—the condition is of course entirely spiritual but let us put it in this way: *we are out of our body*. In this condition we know nothing of the world that lives within us, but we have as it were 'come to ourselves.' We no longer live in the other Beings of the Hierarchies but we live wholly in ourselves. Between death and a new birth we should never have consciousness of ourselves if we lived only in the one condition. Just as here on Earth, inbreathing must alternate with outbreathing, or sleeping with waking life, so between death and a new birth there must be rhythmic alternation between the inner experience of the whole world of the Hierarchies within us, and a condition in which we have come to ourselves.

Now in a certain sense all earthly life is an outcome of what we have experienced in pre-earthly existence between death and a new birth. As you will remember, I have told you how even such faculties in man's earthly life as walking, speaking, and thinking are transformations of certain activities in pre-earthly existence. Today we will turn our attention more specifically to the life of soul.

What we experience in pre-earthly existence in working together with the Beings of the Higher Hierarchies leaves in us a heritage for our earthly life, a faint shadow of this communion with the Hierarchies. If between death and a new birth we had no such community of life with the Beings of the Hierarchies, we could not unfold, here on Earth, the power of *love*. The power of love we unfold here on Earth is of course only a faint reflection, a shadow of our communion with the Spirit-Beings of the Higher Hierarchies between death and a new birth, but it *is* a reflection of that communion. That here on the Earth we are able to unfold human love, sympathetic understanding for another human being, is due to the fact that between death and a new birth we are able to live in communion with the Beings of the Higher Hierarchies.

Spiritual-scientific vision enables us to perceive what happens to those who in previous earthly lives acquired little aptitude—we shall presently speak of *how* it is acquired—for living together during the appropriate period after death with the Beings of the Hierarchies, in certain states entirely given up to them. Such men here on Earth are incapable of unfolding love in which there is real strength, incapable of unfolding that all-embracing love which comes to expression in the power to understand other men. We may say with truth: it is among the Gods, in pre-earthly existence, that we acquire the gift for observing our fellow-man, to perceive how he thinks and how he feels, to understand him with inner sympathy. If we were deprived of this intercourse with the Gods—for so indeed it may be called—we should never be capable of unfolding here on Earth that insight into other human beings which alone makes earthly life a reality. When

51

in this connection I speak of love, and especially of all-embracing human love, you must think of love as having this real and concrete meaning; you must think of it as signifying a genuine, intimate understanding of the other man. If to the all-embracing love of humanity, this understanding of one's fellow-man is added, we have everything that constitutes human *morality*. For human morality on Earth—if it is not merely expressed in empty phrases or fine talk or in resolutions not afterwards carried out—depends upon the interest one man takes in another, upon the capability to see into the other man. Those who have the gift of understanding other human beings will receive from this understanding the impulses for a social life imbued with true morality.

So we may also say: everything that constitutes moral life in earthly existence has been acquired by man in pre-earthly existence; from his communion with the Gods there has remained in him the urge to unfold, in the soul at any rate, community on Earth as well. And it is the development of a life where the one man together with the other fulfils the tasks and the mission of the Earth—it is this alone that in reality leads to the moral life on Earth. Thus we see that love, and the outcome of love—morality—are in very truth a consequence of what man has experienced spiritually in pre-earthly existence.

Now let us think of the other condition in the life between death and rebirth, when man's consciousness of communion with the Beings of the Higher Hierarchies has been dimmed, when, as in earthly sleep, the impressions from the environment are silenced, when deliberate communion with the higher Beings ceases and man 'comes to himself.' This condition too has a consequence, an echo, a heritage, here in earthly life—and this heritage is the faculty of *Memory*.

52

The possibility for us to have experiences at a definite moment and then after a lapse of time to draw forth from the depth of our being something that brings pictures of these experiences into our consciousness—this faculty of memory that is so necessary in our earthly life, is a faint reflection, a shadow, of our *independent* state of life in the spiritual world. Here on Earth we should only be able to live in the passing moment instead of in our whole past life as far back as a few years after birth, if between death and a new birth we were not able to emerge, as it were, from universal life and be entirely alone, alone in ourselves.

While we are asleep here on Earth, our physical and etheric bodies lie in the bed; our astral body and our Ego are outside the physical and the etheric bodies and are then in a position to experience—unconsciously, it is true—the environment of soul and spirit. Man is unconscious between going to sleep and waking. Nevertheless, as I have already said, he does indeed have experiences during sleep, some of which I have also described. But they do not enter the field of consciousness, and in earthly life this is a necessary state of things. What is the reason for it?

If from the time of going to sleep to that of waking we were to experience what we do in fact experience in our Ego and in our astral body, so strongly and intensely as to be able to bring it into consciousness, then every time on waking we should want to impress into the physical and etheric bodies too, what we experienced in sleep; we should want to make our physical and our etheric bodies into something different from what they are. One who has knowledge of what is experienced between going to sleep and waking, must accustom himself to an act of renunciation. He must be able to say to himself: 'I will refrain from the desire to press

53

what I experience with my Ego and my astral body during sleep into the physical and etheric bodies, for in earthly life these bodies could not stand it.'

It is quite possible to speak in a grotesque way about these things—indeed they can be made to seem almost comical, although what is said is meant very seriously. During sleep man does in fact experience images of the Cosmos. Because of this he is continually being tempted, as an outcome of his sleep, to give himself, for example, a different countenance. If that which does not, in fact, come to his consciousness were to do so, he would always be wanting to change his face, for the face he actually has would be reminding him all the time of former earthly lives, of sins in former earthly lives. In the morning, before waking, there is actually a strong urge in man to do to the physical body something that is like dressing it in clothes. One who has knowledge of this must consciously refrain from giving way to the urge; otherwise he would fall into a completely disorganized condition; he would perpetually be trying to change his whole organism, especially if in one respect or another it happens to be not quite healthy, or something is wrong with it.

But during life between death and a new birth we experience so consciously that this consciousness leads to the forming and shaping of our next physical body. If this were left to ourselves alone, we should not shape the physical body in accordance with our karma. In reality, however, we form it together with the Beings of the Higher Hierarchies, the Beings who watch over our karma. And so we get the eyes, the nose, and so forth, which in all probability we should not, if it were left to us, have given to ourselves. For there are certain times between death and a new birth when we are intensely egoistic—precisely at those times when the consciousness of our connection with the Beings of the

Higher Hierarchies has been dimmed. Our experiences are then so strong and intense that out of the forces they contain the physical body can be formed; and we do in fact form it.

This is an experience of such intensity that it has in it the seed of actual creation. Then, through the very fact that it is much weakened in earthly life, it takes effect partly as earthly love and partly as the faculty of remembrance, as memory.

Here on Earth, the fact that we feel ourselves within an Ego, depends upon memory. If we lived only in the present and had no memories, our Ego would have no inner coherence. In fact, as I have often said, we should not be able to feel ourselves in a strongly marked Ego at all. You can understand how memory as an earthly, shadowlike faculty comes into being. It comes into being through the fact that in pre-earthly existence in the spiritual world, a faculty of tremendous power is present—the faculty whereby in those periods when we 'come to ourselves' we prepare our body according to the instructions received from the Beings of the Higher Hierarchies, when, in the other state of existence, we live in union with them.

This faculty is at work, to begin with as a formative force, in our body. In the child, as long as it has no consciousness leading to memory—i.e. in the earliest period of childhood —this stronger creative force still enters into and works with the forces of growth. Then something that is finer, more rarefied, is as it were separated out from these stronger forces—and this is the human faculty of memory.

The fact that here on Earth too man lives primarily in himself, is again connected with this faculty of memory. Memory is also very much connected with human *egoism* on the one side and, on the other, with human *freedom*. Freedom will become a reality in a human being in whose

55

life on Earth there is a true echo of what is experienced in pre-earthly existence as a kind of rhythm: namely, feeling oneself united with the Beings of the Hierarchies, freeing oneself, entering into union again, and so on. Here on Earth the experiences come to expression, not as a rhythm, but as two co-existing human faculties: the faculty of love and the faculty of memory. But a certain heritage from this rhythm in pre-earthly existence can remain with man. If this is so, then in earthly life too the true relationship will be established in him between memory and love. He will be able on the one side to develop understanding, loving understanding of other men. And on the other side, from his experience of the world together with other human beings, his own recollective thinking will contribute to his own development, to the strengthening of his own nature.

A true relationship of this kind *can* remain as a legacy of the rhythm that is an essential in pre-earthly existence. But the true relationship may also be upset. It may, for instance, be that a man is willing to be guided only by what he himself has experienced. This trait is greatly accentuated when a man has little interest in what others experience, little faculty of looking into the hearts and minds of others, when his interest is confined almost entirely to what gradually accumulates in his own store of memories. This again is intimately connected with his Ego, and so egoism is intensified.

Such a man gets 'out of gear' with himself, because the true relationship existing between death and rebirth is lacking in him; a certain rhythm is not there. And at the same time, when a man takes interest only in what piles up in his own soul, when he is concerned all the time with himself alone, then he becomes increasingly unfit—if I may put it so —for the experiences between death and a new birth. By being interested only in himself, a man shuts himself off in a certain respect from communion with the Beings of the Higher Hierarchies.

A man in whom love and memory are rightly interrelated evolves the feeling of true human freedom instead of egoistic introspection. For in another respect this feeling of human freedom too is an echo of the emergence from communion with the Beings of the Higher Hierarchies between death and a new birth. The feeling of freedom is the healthy aftermath of that emergence; egoism is the morbid aftermath. And as the life together with the Beings of the Higher Hierarchies between death and a new birth is the basis of man's morality on Earth, so the necessary emergence from life in communion with them is at the same time the basis on Earth for the immorality of men, for their severance from one another, for actions on the part of the one that cut across the actions of the other, and so forth. For this is at the root of all immorality. So you see it is necessary for man to be mindful that what can appear here on the Earth as something injurious, has a definite significance for the higher worlds. On the Earth too it is the case that the air we inhale is healthy, while the air we exhale is unhealthy, capable of begetting illness, for in effect we exhale carbonic acid. So too, that which underlies immorality here on the Earth is something that is necessary for our experience in the spiritual world.

These connections must be studied because, in effect, morality and immorality cannot really be explained in the light of earthly conditions. Anyone who attempts such explanations will inevitably be on the wrong track. For through the fact that man is moral or the reverse, he relates himself, in his life of soul, to a supersensible world. And we may say: By directing men's minds to the study of this relationship to a spiritual world, anthroposophical Spiritual

57

Science has made it possible, for the first time, to acquire a basis for understanding the *moral*. To a view of the world that will only acknowledge the validity of science dealing with the world of Nature, the moral can only consist in illusions arising from processes of Nature which are supposed to take their course in man as well.

Assume for a moment that the cosmic nebula of Kant and Laplace, with its mechanical forces and mechanical laws, did actually constitute the beginning of Earth-existence; assume that from these whirling nebulae, through the working of neutral laws of Nature, the kingdoms of earthly existence had come into being, and finally Man. If that were so, man's moral impulses would be mere dreams. For everything he calls moral would pass away when, again in accordance with mechanical laws, the Earth had reached her end. No vindication of the reality of the moral life can ever arise from such a world-view if followed honestly to its conclusions. Vindication of the moral can only result when, as in anthroposophical Spiritual Science, those realms of existence are revealed where the moral is as much a reality as the world of Nature is a reality here in the life between birth and death. As plants grow and blossom here, between death and a new birth certain activities unfold when man is among the Gods. These activities are the moral element in its reality, the reality of the moral element. In that realm the moral has reality, whereas on the Earth there is only a reflection of that reality. But man, we must remember, belongs to both worlds. Hence for him, if he can perceive these facts in the light of Spiritual Science, the moral world has reality—but knowledge of this reality can never be derived from physical existence.

Here you have one reason why it is necessary for man to acquire understanding of Spiritual Science. Without Spiritual Science he could not really be honest with his knowledge.

58

He could not honestly ascribe reality to the moral world, because he is not willing to investigate the realm where that reality lies. It is of tremendous importance to understand such a sentence as this in the right way. But there is still another respect in which I want to emphasize how necessary the knowledge attainable through Spiritual Science is to man. Here again we shall have to turn to the realities of another world.

Already when we achieve Imaginative Knowledge—the knowledge that enables us to live in the etheric world instead of in the physical world, so that instead of physical things we perceive the activities (for activities they are) in the ether —already when this is achieved, three-dimensional Space as it is on Earth falls away from our field of experience. To speak of a three-dimensional space has no meaning, for we are then living in *Time*. Hence from from other standpoints I have spoken of the etheric body as a *Time-organism*. I have said, for example, that here, in the spatial organism, we have the head and, let us say, the leg; and if we sting or cut our leg the head will feel it. Spatially, in this spatial body, one organ is connected with the others. So in the time-body which consists in processes—processes in which everything lying in the deeper foundations of our human nature between birth and death are involved—every detail is connected with every other.

You will remember that in lectures on Education I have said that if at a certain age in childhood we have learnt to have reverence, this power of reverence is transformed in later years into a power of gentleness and blessing which can be conveyed to other men. On the other hand, those who in childhood were never able to revere in the true way cannot unfold this power to bless in later life. As in the spatial organism the foot or the leg is connected with the

59

head, so youth is connected with old age, and old age with youth. It is only for external physical vision that the world flows in the one direction, from the past into the future. For higher vision there is also the reverse stream, from the future into the past. It is into this stream, as I have described, that we enter after death, journeying backwards.

In the time-organism everything is interconnected. If the spatial organism as a whole is to be in order, you cannot remove essential organs from it. You cannot, for instance, remove any considerable part of your face without ruining the whole organism. Similarly you cannot remove anything belonging to man that takes its course in time. Imagine that in the spatial organism, at the place where your eyes are situated there were some quite different growth—instead of eyes, some kind of tumor. Then you could not see. As the eyes are situated at a definite place in the spatial organism, so in the time-organism—and I now mean not only the time-organism between birth and death but the time-organism in man that reaches beyond all births and deaths—in this time-organism is incorporated everything that exists between birth and death and in this life develops through concepts, ideas, mental pictures, of a spiritual world. And what thus develops are the eyes for beholding supersensible existence. If between birth and death no knowledge of the supersensible world is developed, this will mean blindness in the life in the supersensible world between death and a new birth, just as the absence of eyes means blindness in the spatial organism. Man passes through death even if on Earth he acquires no knowledge of the supersensible world; but he enters then into a world where he sees nothing, where he can only grope his way about.

This is the agonizing experience that is the natural corollary of the materialistic age for one who has true insight into Initiation-Science today. He sees how men on Earth lapse into materialism; but he also knows what this lapse means for the spiritual life. He knows that it means eradication of the eyes, that in the existence awaiting them after death, men will only be able to grope their way about. In olden times, when there was instinctive knowledge of the supersensible world, men passed through the gate of death able to see. That old, instinctive supersensible knowledge is now extinct. Today, spiritual knowledge must be consciously acquired— *spiritual knowledge,* I say, not clairvoyance. As I have always emphasized, clairvoyance too can be attained, but that is not the essential here. The essential thing is that what is discovered through clairvoyant research shall be understood —as it *can* be understood—by ordinary human reason, healthy human reason. Clairvoyance is needed to investigate these things, but it is *not* needed for acquiring the faculty of sight in the supersensible world after death. And anyone who declares that ordinary knowledge acquired through healthy human reason does not give him eyes for supersensible existence but that for this he needs clairvoyance— anyone who speaks like this might just as well declare that man cannot think unless his eyes do the thinking. As little as in physical life the eyes need think, as little does knowledge of the supersensible worlds need clairvoyance for the purposes I have indicated today.

Naturally, there would be no supersensible knowledge on Earth if there were no clairvoyance; but even the seer must make intelligible in the ordinary way what he sees in the supersensible. However powerful a man's clairvoyant faculty might be in earthly life, however clear his vision of the spiritual world, if he were too easy-going to bring into the form of logical, intelligible ideas what he sees in the spiritual world, he would still be blinded in the spiritual world after death.

What constitutes the great suffering for one who has insight into modern Initiation-Science is that he must admit: materialism makes men blind when they pass through the gate of death. And here again is something showing that it is of significance for the whole of cosmic existence whether man today inclines to supersensible knowledge or not. The time when it is essential for him to do so has arrived; the very progress of humanity depends upon man acquiring supersensible knowledge.

V

Human Faculties and Their Connections with Elemental Beings.

T HE faculties needed by man in order that he may be able to confront the world and work in it during earthly life are connected, as I have shown, with his activities in the spiritual world between death and rebirth. This means, however, that here on Earth man lives in certain spheres which on the Earth itself have no inherent reality, which manifest their reality only when observed in the supersensible realm.

Dornach, December 16, 1922

We will turn our attention today to the three domains which actually comprise all human activity on Earth: to the thoughts through which man endeavors to assimilate *Truth* in the world; to feelings, in so far as in and through his world of feeling, man endeavors to assimilate the *Beautiful*; to his will-nature, in so far as he is meant to bring the *Good* to fulfilment through it.

When we speak of thoughts, we mean that domain through which Truth can be assimilated. But thoughts in themselves cannot be *real*. Precisely when we are clear that through our thoughts we have to inform ourselves about the truth of what is real, then it must also be admitted that thoughts, as such, cannot be anything real. Just imagine for a moment that you were to be fixed as firmly in your thoughts as you are in your brain or your heart; if that were the case, these thoughts would indeed be something real in themselves. We

63

should not be able to assimilate reality through them. Nor could we ever express through human speech what human speech is intended to express if it contained full reality in the ordinary earthly sense. If every time we uttered a sentence we were obliged to work something heavy out of the mouth, we should be unable to *express* anything; it would rather be a matter of *producing* something. In this sense, what is spoken is not a reality in itself, but 'signifies' a reality, just as thoughts are not themselves a reality but merely signify a reality. And if we consider the Good, then we shall find that what is formed through physical reality can never be called the Good. We must bring up from the depths of our being the impulse to Goodness, at first as something entirely unreal, and then make it a reality. If the impulse to Goodness were to arise like hunger, as an external reality, Goodness is just what it could *not* be. Again, when you are looking at a statue it does not occur to you to think that you can converse with it. It is merely semblance; and in the semblance something is made manifest, namely: Beauty. So that in *Truth,* reality is certainly indicated; but Truth itself moves in an element of unreality; and it is the same with *Beauty,* the same with *Goodness.*

It is therefore necessary for man that his thoughts are not, in themselves, real. Just imagine—if thoughts were to wander around in the head like leaden figures, then, to be sure, you would be aware of a reality, but these leaden thoughts would not be able to signify anything to you, they would be something real themselves. As truly as Thoughts, as the Beautiful and the Good too cannot be directly real, so it is also true that reality is necessary in this physical-earthly world in order that we can have Thoughts, make the Beautiful manifest in the world through art, and also bring the Good to fulfilment.

64

In speaking of this I come today to a domain of Spiritual Science which can lead us very deeply into the spirituality that is around us here on Earth and is essential for earthly existence, but completely withdrawn from the observation possible to the senses and hence cannot be grasped by the ordinary consciousness which depends, as you know, entirely upon physical perception. The fact is that we are surrounded everywhere by spiritual beings of the greatest possible variety, only the ordinary consciousness does not perceive them. Their existence is necessary in order that as human beings we may be able to unfold our faculties, to have thoughts in their chimerical lightness and evanescence, so that they are not present in our heads like leaden weights, are not something real in themselves, but can 'signify' reality.

For this it is necessary that there should be beings in the world who prevent our thoughts with their non-reality from immediately vanishing from us again. We men are really too cumbersome, too ponderous, to be able without more ado to hold fast our thoughts with the ordinary consciousness. Elemental beings must be there, beings who help us ever and again to hold fast our thoughts. Such elemental beings are indeed present, only they are extraordinarily hard to discover because they always conceal themselves. When we ask: How does it really come about that we can hold fast a thought when it has no reality at all? Who is helping us to do this?—even then it is very easy to be deceived, precisely when the matter is considered in the light of Spiritual Science. For at the very moment we begin to ask ourselves the question: by whom are thoughts held fast for men?— through this very desire to know about the spirit-entities who hold thoughts fast, we are driven into the realm of the Ahrimanic beings; we plunge into the realm of these beings and very soon begin to believe—although it is of course a deceptive belief—that man must be supported by the Ahrimanic spirits in order to hold fast the thoughts, so that they shall not vanish the moment he grasps them. On this account, most people are—unconsciously—even grateful to the Ahrimanic beings for supporting them in their thinking. But it is misplaced gratitude, for there is a whole kingdom of beings who support us in our thought-world particularly, and who are by no means Ahrimanic.

These beings are difficult to find in the spiritual world, even for well-trained vision. One finds them sometimes by observing a very clever man at work; if one watches such a man one can perceive that he actually has a volatile, fleeting band of followers. He does not go about alone but has a fugitive following of spiritual beings who do not belong to the Ahrimanic kingdom, but who have an altogether remarkable character. One first really learns to know these beings when one can observe those *other* beings who belong to the Ahrimanic realm, to the elemental kingdoms, and therefore are not perceptible to the eyes of the senses, who are at work when forms in Nature, crystal forms, for example, arise. The activity of these beings underlies all form; you find them described in my Mystery Plays as beings who chisel and hammer out solid forms. If you think of the gnome-like beings in one of the Mystery Plays* you have there the beings who produce forms. Now these beings are sly and crafty—as you can see from the way I have presented them in the Play—and they mock at the scanty intelligence possessed by men. Call to mind those scenes from the Mystery Play if they are known to you.

Now if we observe a really clever man and perceive how he may have a retinue consisting of a whole host of such beings as I have described, we find that these beings are

* *The Soul's Awakening.* Scene 2.

despised by the gnome-spirits of the elemental world because they are clumsy and, above all, because they are terribly foolish. Foolishness is their main characteristic! And so it can be said that precisely the very cleverest people in the world, when we can observe them from this aspect, are followed by whole troops of 'spirit-fools.' It is as if these foolish spirits wanted to belong to someone. And they are greatly disdained by the beings who fashion and shape forms in Nature in the way described in the Mystery Plays. We can therefore say: among the worlds unknown to begin with to ordinary consciousness, there is one that is peopled by a spirit-folk of 'fools', fools who throng towards human wisdom and cleverness. In the present age these beings have actually no life of their own. They achieve a life by using the life of those who are dying, who are dying from illness but in whom life-forces are still present. These beings can only make use of a life that is past. Thus there are spirit-fools who use the life that remains over from men; they sate themselves with the life that lingers in cemeteries and such places.

It is when we penetrate into worlds like this that we realize how densely populated is the realm lying behind the world that is perceptible to the senses, how manifold are the classes of spirit-beings, and how closely connected these spirit-beings are with our faculties. A clever man pursuing his activities, who is merely clever and not clairvoyant, can hold fast his thoughts precisely through the fact that he is followed by this troop of spirit-fools. These spirit-fools rivet themselves to his thoughts, drag at them and give them weight, so that they remain with him, whereas otherwise they would quickly vanish from him.

These beings are, as I said, bitterly scoffed at by the gnome-like beings. The gnome-like beings will not tolerate them in their realm although they belong to it. The gnome-like beings drive the others away continually and there is a hard fight between the gnome-folk and this folk of spirit-fools through whom alone wisdom is made possible for man; otherwise the wisdom would be fugitive, would pass away the moment it came into existence, could not remain. As has been said, these beings are hard to discover because it is so easy to fall into the Ahrimanic sphere directly questions are asked about them. But one can find them on occasions such as I have just indicated, by observing very clever men who are followed by a whole troop of such beings. Apart from that, however, when there are not enough clever thoughts fastening on to men, these beings are to be found lingering, for example, in libraries—when the books contain clever material. When the contents of books are stupid these beings are not to be found; they are to be found only where there is cleverness. On that they rivet themselves.

This gives us some insight into a realm that surrounds us everywhere, that is present just as the Nature-kingdoms are present, that has something to do with our faculties, but is very difficult to assess. If we wish to do that we must rely upon those gnome-like beings and set some store by their judgment—and they, in fact, consider the other beings stupid and impudent.

But these other beings have yet another characteristic. When they are too severely persecuted by the gnome-like beings they escape into human heads, and whereas outside in Nature they are almost giants—of an enormous size—they become quite tiny when they are inside men's heads. One could say that they are an abnormal species of Nature-spirits, who are, however, intimately connected with the whole of human evolution on the Earth.

Beings of another kind live chiefly in the watery and airy

elements, just as do those beings described in the Mystery Plays as the sylph-like beings. The beings to whom I am now referring have chiefly to do with the world of 'beautiful semblance.' They attach themselves less to men who are clever in the ordinary sense than to those who are genuinely artistic in nature. But these beings too are very hard to discover as they can so easily conceal themselves. They are to be found where there are genuine works of art, where, for instance, the human form or forms of Nature and so forth are portrayed in semblance. There they are to be found.

These beings too, as I said, can only be discovered with difficulty. When, for instance, we ask: How is it that beautiful semblance interests us, that there are occasions when we derive greater pleasure from a beautiful statue than from a living person (true, it is a different kind of pleasure, but for all that, greater), or that we are edified and delighted by melodies or harmonies? When we ask ourselves this we very easily fall into a different realm, into the realm of the Luciferic beings. It is not only the Luciferic beings who promote enthusiasm for art, but again there is a kingdom of elemental beings by whom interest in art is stimulated and kept alive in man. Without such beings, man would never be disposed to take an interest in beautiful semblance, simply because it is unreal.

Now the reason why it is so difficult to discover these beings is because they can conceal themselves even more easily than the spirit-fools, for they are actually only present where beauty makes its power felt. And when we are wrapt in enjoyment of the beautiful, then we certainly do not see these beings. Why is this?

In order to get a sight of them in a normal way, we must endeavor, while given up in some way to artistic impressions, to direct clairvoyant vision to the beings who are

69

depicted in the same scene in the Mystery Play as nymph- or sylph-like beings; these beings too belong to the elemental Nature-kingdoms, and we must project ourselves into them. We must, as it were, look *with* these air- and water-beings at the others who are present whenever joy is taken in beauty. And as this is difficult, we must turn to other means of help. Now fortunately it is easy to discover these beings when we are listening to someone who speaks beautifully and whose language we do not properly understand; when we hear only the sounds without understanding the meaning. If we then abandon ourselves to the experience of this beautiful speaking—but it must be *really* beautiful speaking, genuine oratory, and we must not be able to understand it properly—then we can acquire the faculty, intimate and delicate as it is, of seeing these beings.

Thus we must try, as it were, to acquire the talent of the sylphs and to strengthen it through the talent that unfolds when we listen to beautiful speech without endeavoring to understand the meaning but having ears only for its beauty. Then we discover the beings who are present wherever beauty is and lend their support so that man can have a true interest in it.

And then follows the disillusionment, the great and terrible surprise. For these beings are in fact hideously ugly, the very ugliest that can be imagined; they are ghastly creatures, the very archetypes of ugliness. And if we have developed the requisite spiritual vision and visit some studio where artistic work is being done, we find that it is these beings who are present on Earth, like spiders on the ground of world-existence, in order that men may take interest in beauty. It is through these frightful spider-creatures of an elemental order that interest in beauty really awakens. Man simply could not have the right interest in beauty if in his life of soul he were not entangled in a world of hideously ugly spider-like beings.

When they are going through a Gallery, people have no inkling—for what I have said refers only to discovering the *form* of these beings, who are always present when anyone is delighting in beauty—people have no inkling of how they are strengthened in the interest they take in beautiful pictures by having these hideous spider-like creatures creeping in and out of their ears and nostrils.

Man's enthusiasm for what is beautiful arises on the foundation of ugliness. That is a cosmic secret, my dear friends. The spur of ugliness is needed in order that the beautiful may be made manifest. And the greatest artists were men who because of their strong bodily constitution could endure the invasions of these spidery beings in order to produce, let us say, a Sistine Madonna, or the like. Whatever beauty is brought forth in the world has been lifted out of a sea of ugliness through the enthusiasm in the human soul.

Let it not be thought that behind the veil of the material world, in the region beyond the threshold, we come into a realm of pure beauty. Do not imagine that anyone who is cognizant of these things speaks lightheartedly when he says that if men are not properly prepared they must be held back at the threshold of the spiritual world. For it is essential first of all to know the thoroughly unedifying foundations of all that in front of the curtain as it were, is uplifting and edifying.

Therefore if with spiritual sight we move about the elemental world belonging to air and water, again we see the great battle waging between the fleeting sylphs and undines and these archetypes of ugliness. Although I spoke of the latter as spidery creatures, the tissues of which they are formed are not like those of spiders as we know them, but

71

they are composed of the elements of water and watery vapor. They are volatile air-formations, the ugliness of which is enhanced inasmuch as every second they have a different ugliness; each succeeding ugliness gives the impression of being even worse than its predecessor. This world is present in air and water together with everything that is delightful there.

And now in order that man may unfold enthusiasm for the Good, something else takes place. It can be said of the other beings that they are more or less actually there, but in the case of the beings of whom I am now going to speak it must really be said that they are continually coming into existence, whenever, in fact, a man has within him warmth of feeling for Goodness. It is in this warmth that these beings develop; their nature itself is warm and fiery; they live in the present but their inherent nature is similar to what I have described in the book *Occult Science* in connection with the Saturn-existence of man.

As man was in the Old Saturn-existence, so are these beings today. Their form is not the same but their nature is similar. It cannot be said of them that they are beautiful or ugly, or anything of that kind; they must be judged in comparison with the ordinary elemental warmth-beings who, as you know, also exist. All spiritual research in this sphere is extraordinarily difficult. It is very difficult to approach the beings who live entirely in warmth, that is to say, in 'fire' in the old sense, and when one does come upon them it is not very pleasant. One comes upon them, for instance, when lying in a high fever, but then as a rule one is not a really objective observer. Otherwise it is a matter of developing the requisite faculty for perceiving these warmth-beings by elaborating the methods indicated in my books. These warmth-beings have a certain relationship with the beings who appear, for instance, when a man has warm enthusiasm for the Good, but the relationship is of a very peculiar kind. I will assume hypothetically—for only in that way can I describe these things—that warmth-beings of the normal kind are present, originating in man's physical warmth, which as you know is greater than the warmth of the environment. Man has his own warmth, hence these particular beings are near him. And now, in a man who has enthusiasm for the Good these *other* beings make themselves manifest; they too are warmth-beings, but of a different kind. When they are in the neighbourhood of the normal fire-beings they immediately draw back from them and slip into the inmost recesses of man's nature. If one then makes great efforts to discover their essential characteristics in contrast to those of the normal warmth-beings, one finds that they have an inner, but very pronounced, bashfulness. They refuse absolutely to be observed by other beings of the spiritual world, and flee from them because they are ashamed of being seen; they flee first and foremost into the inmost nature of man. Hence they are hard to discover. Actually they are only to be discovered if we observe ourselves in certain moments that it is really not so very easy to bring about at will. Just suppose that in spite of not being in the least sentimental we are moved to tears simply by reading a scene in a book that grips us deeply and dramatically. Some great and good action is described, let us say, in a novel. If we have the power of self-observation we can discover how whole hosts of such beings (who have such delicate sensibility that they do not want to be seen by any other beings of the spiritual world) flee into our heart, into our breast, how they come to us, how they seek protection from the other warmth-beings and in fact from any other beings of the elemental spiritual worlds.

There is a significant force of repulsion between the normal warmth-beings and these other warmth beings with their intense bashfulness who live only in the sphere of man's moral life and who flee from contact with other spirit-beings. These beings are present in far greater numbers than is usually imagined and it is they who imbue man with enthusiasm for the morally good. Man would not readily acquire this enthusiasm for the morally good if these beings did not come to his aid; and when a man loves the moral, he has a real bond, an unconscious bond, with these beings.

Certain of their characteristics are such as may lead us to misunderstand this whole kingdom. For after all, why do these beings feel bashful and ashamed? It is actually because all the other beings in the elemental kingdoms of the spiritual world in which they live, disdain them, will have nothing to do with them. They are aware of this and the disdain to which they are subjected causes them to stimulate enthusiasm for the Good.

These beings have certain other characteristics of which I do not care to speak, for the human soul is so obviously upset at any mention of such hideous spidery creatures. I therefore prefer not to refer to certain of their peculiarities. But at any rate we have heard how what unfolds in the realm of the senses as the True, the Beautiful, the Good, unfolds from foundations which need the three spiritual kingdoms I have described, just as we on Earth need the ground on which we walk. These beings do not create the True, the Beautiful or the Good. But the thoughts which express the True, signify the True, need the spirit-dunderheads, so that they may move on their shoulders. The Beautiful that man produces needs the ugly water- and air-spiders so that it can raise itself out of this ocean of ugliness. And the Good needs a kingdom of beings who cannot show themselves at all among the other normal warmth-beings, who must always fight shy of them, and for this very reason evoke enthusiasm for the Good.

If these beings did not exist, then instead of thoughts in our heads we should have, if not exactly leaden soldiers, at least heavy vapors and nothing clever could possibly result. In order to produce the Beautiful we should need to have the gift of imbuing it with actual life in order that men's interest might be aroused. In order that here, in the world of the senses, there may be at hand what we need for the activity of thought, for the sense of beauty, for the will to arouse enthusiasm for the good—for this, three such elemental kingdoms are necessary.

The normal elemental kingdoms—that is, the kingdoms of the gnomes, sylphs, undines and salamanders, to use folk-terminology—are still at the stage of striving to become something in the world. They are on the way to having forms resembling those in our sense-world; the forms will not be the same, but one day they will become perceptible to the senses possessed by men today, whereas now, in their elementary existence, these beings are not perceptible to the ordinary senses.

The beings I have now described to you have in fact already by-passed the stage at which men and animals and plants are today. So that if, for example, we were able to go back to the Old Moon-existence which preceded the Earth, we should there encounter the beings found on Earth today as the bashful beings connected with moral impulses in man. On the Old Moon they would have been perceptible as a real animal world, spinning as it were from tree to tree. But you must call to mind the Old Moon-existence as I have described it in the book *Occult Science*. Everything in this Moon-existence was pliable and fluid and metamorphosis has continually taken place. Among the beings there, spinning in and out, were those hideous beings I have described, those spidery creatures permeating the Old Moon and visible there. And there were also present the beings who as spirit-fools accompany the wise on the Earth today. They were a factor in bringing about the destruction of the Old Moon, so that the Earth could arise. And even now, during Earth-existence, these beings have no pleasure in the formation of crystals, but rather in the breaking up of everything mineral.

Thus while we can say of the normal elemental beings that they will one day become visible to the senses, we must say of these other beings: once upon a time they were visible to the senses and have now sprung over into the spiritual—admittedly through their Luciferic and Ahrimanic natures. Thus there are two kinds of elemental beings—ascending and descending. We can say: on the 'dung' of Old Moon ugliness—which was there in profusion during the Old Moon-existence—on the 'dung' of Old Moon ugliness, our world of beauty springs forth.

You have an analogy in Nature when you carry manure to the fields and beautiful plants spring from it. There you have an analogy in Nature except that the dung, the manure, is also perceptible to the senses. So it is when the half-reality of the world of beauty is observed clairvoyantly. Try to envisage this half-real world of beauty, quite apart from the teeming life in the three kingdoms of Nature on the Earth; picture all the beautiful after-effects springing from the Earth. Just as lovely flowers spring up in a meadow, you must spiritually picture underneath it all the Moon-dung which contains the ugly spidery creatures I have described. Just as cabbage does not grow unless it is manured, as little can beauty blossom on the Earth unless the Gods manure the Earth with ugliness. That is the inner necessity of life. And this inner necessity of life must be known to us, for such knowledge alone can give us the power to confront with understanding what actually surrounds us in Nature.

Anyone who believes that beauty in art can be produced on Earth without the foundation of this ugliness is like a man who is horrified that people use manure, insisting that it would be far better to let beautiful things grow without it.— In point of fact it is not possible for beauty to be produced without the foundation of ugliness. And if people do not want to give themselves up to illusion about the world, that is, if they genuinely desire to know the essential and not the illusory, then they must acquire knowledge of these things. Whoever believes that there is art in the world without ugliness does not know what art is. And why not? Simply for the reason that only he who has an inkling of what I have described to you today will enjoy works of art in the right way, for he knows at what cost they are purchased in world-existence. Whoever wants to enjoy works of art without this consciousness is like a man who would prefer to do away with manure on the fields. Such a man has no real knowledge of what grows in Nature; he has, in fact, merely an illusion before him—plants of *papier-maché,* although real plants are actually there. Whoever does not feel ugliness as the foundation has not the right kind of delight in beauty.

Such is the world-order and men must acquire knowledge of it if they do not want to go on wandering about like earthworms, keeping to their own element and not looking upwards to what is real. Men can only develop the talents latent within them if they confront reality fairly and squarely. Reality, however, is not attained merely by talking time and time again of spirit, spirit, spirit, but by really coming to know the spiritual. But the fact has also to be faced that in certain regions of the spiritual world something like I have been describing to you today will be encountered.

VI

Spiritualization of Knowledge of Space.
The Mission of Michael.

Dornach, December 17, 1922

I HAVE often referred to the fact that since about the first third of the fifteenth century, human evolution has entered upon a special epoch. It can be said that the age which began approximately in the eighth century B.C. and continued into the first third of the fifteenth century was the age of Graeco-Latin culture and that the most recent phase of time in which we are still living today, began at the point I have indicated. Today we will consider the tasks of present-day humanity in connection with this fact.

We know—particularly from the lectures given here lately —that between birth and death man bears in his physical, psychical and spiritual development on Earth the heritage of what he has experienced in pre-earthly existence. And recently we heard in what sense social and moral life is the heritage of that condition between death and rebirth when man lives in intimate communion with the Beings of the Higher Hierarchies. From this communion—it is experienced, as I have described, in rhythmic alternation with another condition—man brings with him the power of love, and this power of love is the foundation of morality on Earth. The other condition is the one in which man withdraws into himself, when, as it were, he lifts himself out of this communion with the Beings of the Hierarchies. And as the heritage of this condition he brings with him to Earth the power of memory, the power of remembrance, which on the one side comes to expression in his egoism, but on the other side predisposes him for freedom, for everything that makes for inner strength and independence.

Until the Graeco-Latin epoch, the faculties that enabled man to shape his civilization from within were in a certain respect still a heritage of pre-earthly existence.

If we go back to still earlier times in the evolution of humanity, to the Old Indian, the Old Persian and the Egyptian epochs, we find evidence everywhere of knowledge, of ideas, which flow as it were out of man's inner being but are also connected with the life between death and rebirth. In the Old Indian epoch man has a clear consciousness that he belongs to the same 'race' to which the divine-spiritual Beings of the Hierarchies belong. A man of knowledge in ancient Indian civilization feels himself less a citizen of the Earth than of the world to which these divine-spiritual Beings belong. He feels that he has been sent down to the Earth from the ranks of these divine-spiritual Beings. And he considers that the civilization he spreads over the Earth is there in order that the earthly deeds of man and even the objects and beings of the Earth may conform with the nature of the divine-spiritual Beings to whom he feels himself related.

In the man of ancient Persia this feeling of kinship has already lost some of its former intensity but he too still feels his real home to be what he called the Kingdom of Light, the Kingdom to which he belongs between death and rebirth, and he desires to be a warrior on the side of the spirits of this Kingdom of Light. He wishes to fight against those beings who come from the darkness of the Earth so that the spirits of the Kingdom of Light may not be hampered by these dark beings; he dedicates all his activity to the service

79

of the spirits of the Kingdom of Light. And if we then pass on to the Egyptian and Chaldaean peoples we see how their science is full of knowledge relating to the movements of the stars. The destinies of men are read from what the stars reveal. Before anything is done on Earth, the stars are asked whether it would or would not be justified. This science, according to which all earthly life is regulated, is likewise felt to be a heritage of man's existence between death and rebirth, when his experiences are of a kind that make him one with the movements and laws of the stars, just as here on Earth between birth and death he is one with the beings of the mineral, plant and animal kingdoms.

In the fourth post-Atlantean, the Graeco-Latin epoch, beginning in the eighth century B.C. and lasting until the fifteenth century A.D., men already feel themselves to be true citizens of the Earth. They feel that in their world of ideas between birth and death there are no longer very distinct echoes of experiences in pre-earthly existence. They strive to be at home on the Earth. And yet, if we penetrate deeply into the spirit of Greek and even of early Roman civilization we can say something like the following. The men who are founding science in that age are intent upon learning to know all that goes on in the three kingdoms of Nature upon Earth, but to know it in such a way that this knowledge also has some relation to extra-terrestrial existence. Among the Greeks there is a strong feeling that through the knowledge applied by man on the Earth and in the light of which he regulates his earthly deeds, he should at the same time have a dim remembrance of the divine-spiritual world. The Greek knows that he can gain his knowledge only from observation of the earthly world; but he has a clear feeling that what he perceives in the minerals, in the plants, in the animals, stars, mountains, rivers, and so forth, must be a reflection of the Divine-Spiritual which he can experience in a world other than the world of the senses.

This is the case because in that epoch man still feels that with the best part of his being he belongs to a supersensible world. This supersensible world has, to be sure, become darkened for human observation—that is how man puts it to himself—but during earthly existence too he must strive to illumine it. True, in the Graeco-Latin epoch men can no longer regulate the ordinary deeds of humanity in accordance with the courses of the stars, since their mastery of the science of the stars is not on a par with that of the Chaldaean and the Egyptians; but at all events they still endeavor, rather gropingly, through studying expressions of the will of the divine-spiritual Beings, to bring something of the Divine-Spiritual into the earthly world.

In places of the Oracles and in Temples, men sought to ascertain the will of the Gods from priestesses and prophetesses, as you know from history. And we see how these endeavors to ascertain the will of the divine-spiritual Beings with whom man himself is one during pre-earthly existence, were also customary in other regions of Europe at the time when Graeco-Roman culture was in its prime in the South. In the Germanic regions of Middle Europe, for example, priestesses and prophetesses were highly venerated; pilgrimages were made to them and in ecstatic states of consciousness, the will of the Gods was made known to men so that their deeds on Earth might be in conformity with this will. We can see quite clearly how up to the twelfth and thirteenth centuries—although the urge is by then less intense—man strives to formulate the knowledge he seeks in such a way that it contains within it the will of the divine-spiritual world. Through these centuries of the Middle Ages, right up to the twelfth and thirteenth, we can find places which at that time were still considered sacred and later became our laboratories—we can find places where the so-called alchemists were investigating the forces of substances and of Nature-processes; we can peruse writings which still give a faint picture of the kind of thinking that was applied in those old centres of research and we shall everywhere discover evidence of the striving to bring the substances themselves into such combinations or mutual interaction that the Divine-Spiritual can work in the phial, in the retort.

In Goethe's *Faust* there is an echo of this attitude of soul, in the scene where Wagner is working in his laboratory to produce Homunculus. It is really not until the turn of the fourteenth and fifteenth centuries in Western civilization that the desire arises in man to lay the foundations of a science in complete independence, without bringing his ideas into any direct connection with a divine-spiritual will by which the world is ruled. A purely human form of knowledge arises for the first time during this period; it is knowledge that is emancipated from the divine-spiritual will. And it is this purely human knowledge, emancipated from the divine will of which the science of Galileo and Copernicus is composed. It is science through which the universe is presented to man in the abstract picture current today, the picture of a vault —as Giordano Bruno was the first to envisage—with the stars circling in it as purely material bodies, or even in a condition of rest taking their share in cosmic happenings. This picture of the universe makes us imagine that a vast mechanism works in upon the Earth from cosmic space. And even in the investigation of earthly things people confine themselves fundamentally to what can be calculated and measured and so be part of an abstract mechanism. This, however, is a world of conceptions and ideas which man can spin out of himself with the help of external observation and

82

experiment, where the physical substances alone are believed to affect each other, the Nature-processes to become manifest and where the Divine-Spiritual is no longer sought in the world of Nature.

There is a vast difference between this conceptual world and the kind of thought that preceded it in human evolution. It is only since the first third of the fifteenth century that man's concepts and ideas have become purely human. And it is the *spatial* with which man has mainly concerned himself since this period began.

If you go back still farther to the times of the Old Indian, the Old Persian, the Egypto-Chaldaean culture, everywhere you will find that world-conceptions refer to World *Ages*. They point back to an ancient epoch when mankind still had intercourse with the Gods, to a Golden Age. They point back to another epoch when man still experienced on Earth at least the sun-reflection of the Divine—a Silver Age, and so on. *Time* and the course of Time play a conspicuous role in the world-pictures of early evolutionary phases. Likewise, when you consider the Greek epoch, and indeed the world-picture that was current at the same time in the more Northerly and Middle European regions, you will find that everywhere the idea of Time plays an essential part. The Greek points back to that primeval Age when cosmic happenings are the outcome of interaction between Uranus and Gaia. He points to the next Age, to Chronos and Rhea, then to the Age when Zeus and the other Gods known in Greek Mythology rule the Cosmos and the Earth. And it is the same in Germanic Mythology. Time plays the most essential role in all these world-pictures.

A much less important part is played by *Space*. The spatial element is still obscure in the Norse and Germanic world-pictures with the World Ash, the Giant Ymir and so forth.

That something is taking place in Time is quite clear, but the idea of Space is only dimly dawning; it is a factor of no great significance. It is not until the age of Galileo, of Copernicus, of Giordano Bruno, that Space actually begins to play its great role in the picture of the universe. Even in the Ptolemaic system which admittedly is concerned with Space, Time is a more essential factor than it is in the world-picture familiar to us since the fifteenth century, in which Time actually plays a secondary part. The present distribution of the stars in cosmic space is taken as the starting-point and through calculation conclusions are reached as to what the world-picture was like in earlier times. But the conception of Space, the spatial world-picture, becomes of chief importance. And the result is that all human judgments are based on the principle of Space. Modern man has elaborated this element of Space in his external world-picture, elaborated it too in all his thinking. And today this thinking in terms of Space has reached its zenith.

Think how difficult it is for a man of the present day to follow an exposition purely of Time. He is happy if Space is brought in at least to the extent of drawing something on the blackboard. But if the feeling of Space is conveyed by means of photographs, then the modern man is verily in his element! "Illustration"—and by this he means expression in terms of *Space*—is what man of today strives to achieve in every exposition. Time, inasmuch as it is in perpetual flow, has become something that causes him discomfort. He still attaches value to it in music; but even there the tendency towards the spatial is quite evident.

We need only consider something that has become a definite feature of modern life and this mania of modern man to cleave to the spatial is at once apparent. In the cinema he is utterly indifferent to the element of Time in the picture. He is content with the merest fraction of the Time element and is entirely given up to the element of Space.

This orientation of the soul to the spatial is very characteristic of the present time and whoever observes modern culture and civilization with open eyes will find it everywhere.

On the other hand, in anthroposophical Spiritual Science we are striving, as you know, to get away from the spatial. To be sure, we meet the desire for it in that we too try to give tangible form to the spiritual, and that is justifiable in order to strengthen the faculty of ideation. Only we must always be conscious that this is purely a means of illustration and that what is essential is to strive, at least to strive, to transcend the spatial.

Space 'devotees' among us often cause difficulties by making diagrams of the consecutive epochs of Time, writing "First Epoch with Sub-Epochs," and so on. Then follow a great many captions and what is sequential in Time is dragged into a spatial picture.

Our aim, however, is to transcend the spatial. We are striving to penetrate into the temporal and also into the super-temporal, into the element that leads beyond what is physically perceptible. The physically perceptible exists in its crudest form in the world of Space and there thought is led in a certain direction. I have often spoken of the real intentions of anthroposophical Spiritual Science. It certainly does not belittle, let alone reject, the mode of thinking engendered in the age of Galileo, Copernicus, Giordano Bruno. The validity of this mode of thinking in which, as you know, Space is the essential element, is fully recognized by anthroposophical Spiritual Science. Therefore it ought to be able to shed light into every domain of scientific

85

thought. It must not adopt an amateurish attitude to these domains of scientific thought but must shed light into them by its way of looking at things.

But over and over again it must be stressed that anthroposophical Spiritual Science is endeavoring to guide back again to the Divine-Spiritual this purely human knowledge that is based almost entirely on the element of Space and is emancipated from the Divine-Spiritual. We do not hark back to ancient conditions but we desire to guide the modern attitude of soul into the spiritual, away from its preoccupation with what is purely spatial and material. In other words, we want to learn to talk about *spiritual* things, as people in the Galileo-Copernican age grew accustomed to talk about substances, about forces. With its methods of study and observation, this Spiritual Science is to be a match for the kind of knowledge that has been developing in connection with the things and processes of the material world since the first third of the fifteenth century. Its aim is the attainment of spiritual knowledge that is related to this Nature-knowledge, although since the former is concerned with the supersensible, the contrast is very apparent.

Inwardly considered, what is it that we are seeking to achieve? If we transfer ourselves in thought into the position of the divine-spiritual Beings in whose ranks we live between death and rebirth, and discern how they direct their gaze downwards, and through the various means I have described observe the course of events on Earth, then we find that these Beings looked down to the Earth in the earlier ages of human evolution—in the Old Indian, Old Persian, Old Chaldaean-Egyptian epochs—and beheld what men were doing, what views they held of Nature and of their own social life. And then—if I may put it so—the Gods were able to say to themselves concerning the deeds and thoughts of men: Their deeds and their thoughts are a result of their memory of, or are an echo of, what they experienced among us in our world.—In the case of the Chaldaeans or Egyptians it was still quite evident that the primary wish of men below on the Earth was to carry out what the Gods above had thought or were thinking. When the Gods looked down to the Earth they beheld happenings that were in keeping with their intentions; and it was the same when they looked into the thoughts of men—as Gods are able to do. Since the first third of the fifteenth century this has changed. Since then, the divine-spiritual Beings have looked down to the Earth, and especially when they look down at the present time, they find that things everywhere are fundamentally alien to them, that men are doing things on the Earth which they themselves have planned in accordance with the phenomena and processes of earthly existence. And to the Gods with whom men live between death and rebirth, this is an entirely alien attitude.

When an alchemist in his laboratory was endeavoring to ascertain the divine-spiritual will through the combination and separation of the Elements, a God would have beheld something akin to his own nature in what the alchemist was doing. If a God were to look into a modern laboratory, the methods and procedure adopted there would be intensely alien to him. It can be said with absolute truth that since the first third of the fifteenth century, the Gods have felt as if the whole human race had fallen away from them in a certain respect, as if men down on the Earth were engaged in self-made trivialities, in things which the Gods are unable to understand,—certainly not the Gods who still guided the hands and minds of men in their scientific pursuits in Graeco-Latin times. These divine-spiritual Beings have no active interest in what is done in modern laboratories, let alone in modern hospitals. I was obliged on a previous occasion to say that when the Gods look down through windows, as I called them, what interests them least of all on Earth is the kind of work carried out by professors. What goes to the very heart of one who has genuine insight into modern Initiation Science is that he is obliged to say to himself: In recent times we men have become estranged from the Gods; we must seek again for bridges to connect us with the divine-spiritual world.—And it is this that quickens the impulse for anthroposophical Spiritual Science. Its desire is to transform the scientific ideas and concepts that are unintelligible to the Gods in such a way that they are spiritualized and are thus able to provide a bridge to the Divine-Spiritual.

It should be realized that light, for example, is something in which divinity is present. This was strongly felt in ancient Persian culture, but today when, for example, attempts are made to indicate by all sorts of lines how the rays from a lens are broken, this is a language that the Gods do not understand; it means nothing at all to them. All these things must be approached by an attitude of soul that enables the bridge to the Divine to be found once again. To realize this means a great deepening of insight into the kind of task that is incumbent upon the present age in the matter of transforming and metamorphosing our unspiritual ideas.

A cosmic truth of deep significance underlies these things. The conception of Space is an entirely human conception. The Gods with whom man lives together in the most important period of his life between death and a new birth have a vivid conception of Time but no conception of Space such as man acquires on Earth. This conception of Space is entirely human. Man really enters into Space for the first time when he descends from the divine-spiritual world into the physical world of the Earth. True, as seen from here, everything appears in spatial perspective. But thinking in dimensions, if I may put it so, is something that belongs entirely to the Earth.

In Western civilization this conception of Space has become ingrained in man since the fifteenth century. But when through the spiritualizing of purely spatial knowledge, bridges to the divine world have been found again, then what man has gained from the science of Space—in the very period when he has emancipated his thought most drastically from the divine world, i.e. since the fifteenth century—all the spatial knowledge he has gained will become important for the divine-spiritual world as well. And man can conquer a new portion of the universe for the Gods if he will but bring the spirit again into the conception of Space.

You see, what I have described in the book *Occult Science* —the periods of Old Saturn, Old Sun, Old Moon, Earth and the future periods of Jupiter, Venus, Vulcan—is only present to the Gods in the sequence of *Time*. Here on Earth, however, it all lives itself out in terms of Space. We are living today in the Earth period proper but in happenings on the Earth there still linger the echoes of the periods of Old Moon, Old Sun and Old Saturn.

If you will steep yourselves in the description of the Old Saturn period given in *Occult Science*, you will say: The Saturn period is past but the effects of its warmth are still present in our earthly existence. Saturn, Sun, Moon, Earth are within one another; they exist simultaneously. The Gods see them in the sequence of *Time*. Although in earlier ages, even during Chaldaean times they were seen in their succession, now we see them within one another, spatially within one another. Indeed this leads very much farther and if we study these things in detail, we shall discover what really lies behind them.

89

Imagine that you stretch out your left hand. The Divine lives in everything terrestrial. In your muscles, in your nerves, lives the Divine. Now with the fingers of your left hand you touch the fingers of your right hand—this can only be done *in Space*. The fact that you feel your right hand with your left, your left hand with your right—this is something which the divine-spiritual Beings do not follow. They follow the left hand and right hand up to the point of contact, but the feeling that arises between the two is an experience which the faculties possessed by the Gods do not make possible; it is something that arises only in Space. Just as little as the Gods behold Saturn, Sun, Moon and Earth simultaneously but only in succession, in Time, so they have none of the purely spatial experiences known to man. When you look with your left and right eyes and have the lines of vision from right and from left, the activity of the Gods is present in the vision from the right eye and again in the vision from the left eye, but in the *meeting* of the two lines of vision lies the purely human element. Thus we experience as men, because we have been placed into the world of Space, something that is experienced in a state of emancipation from the activity of the Gods.

You need only extend this imagery of the right and left hands to other domains in the life of earthly man, and you will find a great many human experiences that fall right away from the Gods' field of vision. It is really only since the first third of the fifteenth century that man has brought ideas of a purely human kind into these domains. Hence human thinking has become less and less intelligible to the Gods when they look down to the Earth. And with this in mind we must turn our attention to that most important event in the last third of the nineteenth century which may be characterized by saying that the rulership of the Spiritual

Being known as Gabriel was succeeded by the rulership of that other Spiritual Being known as Michael.

In the last third of the nineteenth century the Spiritual Being we call Michael became the Ruler, as it were, of everything of a spiritual character in human events on the Earth. Whereas Gabriel is a Being orientated more to the passive qualities of man, Michael is the active Being, the Being who as it were pulses through our breath, our veins, our nerves, to the end that we may actively develop all that belongs to our full humanity in connection with the Cosmos. What stands before us as a challenge of Michael is that we become active in our very thoughts, working out our view of the world through our own inner activity. We only belong to the Michael Age when we do not sit down inactively and desire to let enlightenment from within and from without come to us, but when we co-operate *actively* in what the world offers us in the way of experiences and opportunities for observation. If a man carries out some experiment, it does not fundamentally involve activity; there is not necessarily any activity on his part; it is just an event like any other event in Nature, except that it is directed by human intelligence. But all happenings in Nature have also been directed by intelligence! How is man's mental life nowadays affected by experiments? There is no active participation, for he simply looks on and tries to eliminate activity as much as possible; he wants to let the experiment tell him everything and regards as fanciful anything that is the outcome of his own inner activity. It is precisely in their scientific ideas that men are least of all in the Michael Age.

But humanity *must* enter into the Michael Age. If we put the question to ourselves: What does it actually mean in the whole cosmic setting that Gabriel should have passed on the sceptre to Michael?—then we must answer: It means that

91

of all the Beings who spiritually guide humanity, Michael is the Spirit who is the first to draw near to what men here on Earth are doing as the result of this emancipation of knowledge since the first third of the fifteenth century. Gabriel stands in utter perplexity before the ideas and notions of a cultured man of the modern age. Michael, who is closely connected with the forces of the Sun, can at least instil his activity into such thoughts of man as can be impulses for his free deeds. Michael can work, for instance, into what I have called in *Occult Science,* free, pure thinking, which must be the true impulse for the individual will of man acting in freedom in the new age. And with the deeds of man which spring from the impulse of love, Michael has his own particular relationship.

Hence he is the messenger whom the Gods have sent down so that he may receive what is now being led over from knowledge emancipated from spirit into spiritualized knowledge. The science which as anthroposophical Spiritual Science again spiritualizes spatial thinking, lifts it again into the supersensible—this Spiritual Science works from below upwards, stretches out its hands as it were from below upwards to grasp the hands of Michael stretching down from above. It is then that the bridge can be created between man and the Gods. Michael has become the Regent of this Age because he is to receive what the Gods wish to receive from what man can add to the Time-concept through the Space-concept—for this augments the knowledge possessed by the Gods.

The Gods picture Saturn, Sun, Moon, Earth, in the succession of Time. If man rightly develops the latest phase of his life of thought, he sees this in terms of Space. The Gods can picture the outstretching of the left and of the right hand, but the actual contact is a purely human matter. The Gods can live in the line of vision of the left eye, in the line of vision of the right eye. Man envisages in terms of Space how the vision of the left eye meets that of the right eye. Michael directs his gaze down upon the Earth. He is able, by entering into connection with what men develop in pure thought and objectify in pure will, to take cognisance of what is acquired by the citizens of Earth, by men, as the fruit of thinking in terms of Space, and to carry it up into divine worlds.

If men were merely to develop Space-knowledge and not spiritualize it, if they were to stop short at Anthropology and were not willing to advance to Anthroposophy, then the Michael Age would go by. Michael would retire from his rulership and would bring this message to the Gods: Humanity desires to separate itself from the Gods.—If Michael is to bring back the right message to the world of the Gods, he must speak to this effect: During my Age, men have raised to the Supersensible what they have already developed in the way of thinking purely in terms of Space; and we can therefore accept men again, for they have united their thought with ours.—If human evolution proceeds in the right way, Michael will not have to say to the Gods: Men have become accustomed to stare at everything spatially; they have learnt to despise what lives only in Time.—If human beings are resolved to achieve their earthly goal, Michael will say: Men have made efforts to bring Time and the Supersensible again into the Spatial; therefore those who are not content merely to stare at the Spatial, who are not content to accept everything in such a material form as was customary at the beginning of the twentieth century, can be regarded as having linked their lives directly to the life of the Gods.—

If we genuinely pursue Anthroposophy in the light of Initiation Science, it means that we concern ourselves with cosmic affairs, with affairs which humanity has to work out in harmony with the world of the Gods. And in the present age very much is at stake; it is a matter of whether we shall or shall not sow the seed for true communion in the future with the divine-spiritual world.

When you realize the tremendous significance of this issue, you will be able to measure the earnestness and inner steadfastness needed by the soul if Anthroposophy is to be the content of its life of thought.

VII

Inner Processes in the Human Organism.
Sense-Perception, Breathing, Sleeping,
Waking, Memory.

Dornach, December 22, 1922

MAN perceives the things of the world through his senses but with his ordinary consciousness he does not perceive what takes place *within* the senses themselves. Were he to do this in everyday life he would not be able to perceive the outer world. The senses must, as it were, renounce themselves if they are to bring to man's cognizance what lies outside the senses in the world immediately surrounding him on Earth. If our ear could speak or our eye could speak, if we could by this means become aware of the processes taking place in those organs, we should not be able to hear what is outwardly audible nor see what is outwardly visible. But it is precisely this that enables man to know the world round about him, in so far as he is an Earth-being; he does not, however, thereby learn to know *himself*. This presupposes that during the process of acquiring self-knowledge one is able to suspend all cognition of the outer world, so that for a time nothing at all is experienced from the external world.

In Spiritual Science it has always been the endeavor to discover methods through which man may acquire true self-knowledge, and you are aware from the many different lectures I have given, that by this self-knowledge I do not mean the ordinary kind of brooding contemplation of the everyday self; for all that a man experiences thereby is simply a reflex picture of the external world. He learns nothing that is new;

he merely gets to know, as it were in a mirror, what he has experienced in the outer physical world. True self-knowledge must, as you know, proceed through methods which silence not only the earthly outer world, but also the everyday soul-content which, as it exists in actual consciousness, is simply a mirror-picture of the outer world. And through the methods described in the book *Knowledge of the Higher Worlds and Its Attainment,* you know that spiritual research advances first to what is called Imaginative Cognition. Whoever advances to this Imaginative Cognition has before him, to begin with, everything from the supersensible world that can clothe itself in the images and pictures of this form of higher knowledge. And when he has acquired the inner faculty of Imaginative vision of the world, he is in a position to follow what takes place in the human sense-organs.

It would not be possible to follow what takes place in the sense-organs if something were to go on there only while the outer world were being perceived through them. When I am seeing an object of the outer world, my eye is still. When I am hearing some sound of the outer world my ear is still. This means that what the ear becomes aware of is not what goes on within the ear itself but what is continuing from the external world into the ear. But if, for example, the ear were only to be active in connection with the external world as long as outer perception were taking place, we should never be able to observe the process that goes on in the ear itself, independently of the outer world. But you all know that a sense-impression has an after-effect in the senses, apart from the fact that the senses always take part even when we are merely thinking actively in our ordinary consciousness.

It is possible to withdraw entirely from the external world in so far as it is a world of color, of sound, of smell, and so

96

forth, and give attention only to what goes on within, or by means of, our sense-organs themselves. When we reach this point we have taken the first step towards acquiring true knowledge of man. To take the simplest example, let us say we want to understand how an impression made upon the eye from outside dies away. A person who has acquired the faculty of Imaginative Cognition is able, because he is perceiving nothing in the external world, to follow this dying away of the sense-impression. That is to say, he is following a process in which the sense-organ as such is involved, although at this moment it is actually not in connection with the external world. Or, let us say, someone can picture vividly to himself something he has seen, realizing how the organ of sight participated in the living thought of the colors, and so on. The same can be done in the case of all the senses. Then such a person actually becomes aware that what takes place within the senses themselves can only be perceived by Imaginative Cognition. A world of Imaginations appears before our soul as if by magic when we live, not in the external world, but *in* the senses themselves. And then we realize that our senses actually belong to a world other than the one we perceive through them in our Earth-existence. Nobody who is truly in a position, through the acquisition of Imaginative Knowledge, to observe the activity of his own senses, can ever doubt that man, as a being of sense, belongs to the supersensible world.

In the book *Occult Science,* I have called the world that man learns to know by thus withdrawing his attention from the outer world and living within his own senses, the world of the *Angeloi,* the Beings who stand one stage higher than man. What is it that actually happens in our senses? We can fathom it if we are able to observe the inner activity of the senses while we are not actually perceiving with them.

Just as we can remember an experience that took place years before, although it is no longer present, so, if we are able to observe the senses while they are not engaged in any act of perception, we can acquire knowledge of what happens there. It cannot be called remembrance, for that would convey a fallacious idea; nevertheless, in what we perceive we can at the same time perceive the processes that are engendered in the senses by the outer world through color, sound, smell, taste, touch, and so forth.

In this way we can penetrate into something of which man is otherwise unconscious, namely, the activity of his own senses while the outer world is transmitting its impressions to him. And here we become aware that the breathing process—the inbreathing of the air, the distribution of the air in the human organism, the outbreathing—works in a remarkable way through the whole organism. When we breathe in, the inhaled air passes into the very finest ramifications of the senses, and here the rhythmical breathing comes into contact with what is called in Spiritual Science, the astral body of man. What goes on in the senses depends upon the astral body coming into contact with the rhythmical breathing process. Thus when you hear a tone, it is because in your organ of hearing the astral body can come into contact with the vibrating air. It cannot do this in any other part of the human organism, but only in the senses. The senses are present in man in order that the astral body can contact what arises in the human body through the breath. And this happens not only in the organ of hearing but in every sense-organ; even in the sense of touch or feeling that extends over the whole organism the astral body actually comes in contact with the rhythmical breathing, that is to say, with the action of the air in our organism.

It is precisely when studying these things that we realize

how necessary it is to keep in mind that man is not merely a solid structure, but almost 90% a column of water; as the air circulates all the time in the inner processes of his body, he is also an air-organism. And the air-organism, with its weaving life, comes into contact, in the sense-organs, with man's astral body. This takes place in very manifold ways in the sense-organs, but speaking generally it may be said that this meeting is the essential factor in all sensory processes.

To observe how an astral body comes into contact with the air is not possible unless we enter the Imaginative world. With Imaginative Cognition other conditions are perceived in the environment of the Earth where the astral forces come into contact with the air. But within us as human beings, what is of essential importance is that the astral body comes into contact with the breathing process and with what is actually sent by the breathing process through the bodily organism.

Thus we learn to know the weaving activity of the Beings belonging to the hierarchy of the Angeloi. The only true picture we can have of it is that in the unconscious process which takes its course in sense-perception, this world of supersensible Beings is working and weaving, passing in and out, as it were, through the doors of our senses. When we hear and when we see, this is a process that does not take place only through our arbitrary will, but belongs also to the objective world, operating in a sphere where we men are not even present, yet through which we are truly men, men endowed with senses.

You see, when our astral body between waking and falling asleep enters into relation in the sphere of our senses with the air that has now become rhythmical breathing and has therefore changed in character, we learn, so to say, to know the outermost periphery of man. But we learn to know still more of man if we can reach the higher stage of supersensible cognition called Inspiration in the books already mentioned.

At this point we must think of how man is subject to the alternating states of waking and sleeping life. Sense-perception too is subject to alternation. Perceptions would not have the right effect upon our consciousness if we were not able continually to interrupt the process involved. You know from purely external experiences that prolonged surrender to a sense-perception impairs consciousness of it. We must again and again withdraw from a given sense-impression, that is to say, we must alternate between the impression and a condition when we have no impression. For our consciousness to be normal as regards sense-impressions depends upon our being able also to withdraw the senses from the impression that is being made upon them; sense-perception must always be subject to these brief alternating conditions. These alternations also occur in longer periods of our life, for we alternate once in every twenty-four hours between waking and sleeping.

You are aware that when we pass over into the condition of sleep, our astral body and ego leave our physical and etheric bodies. Consequently between going to sleep and waking the astral body enters into relation with the outer world, whereas between waking and going to sleep it is related only to what goes on within the human body. Picture to yourselves these two states, or these two processes: the astral body between waking and going to sleep in connection with what occurs within the human physical and etheric bodies, and the astral body between going to sleep and waking in connection with the outer world, no longer with the physical and etheric bodies of man himself.

The spheres of the senses in us are already almost an outer world—if I may use an expression which, though paradoxical, you will understand. Think, for example, of the human eye. It is like an independent being—naturally I mean this only analogously—but it is truly like an independent being placed there in a cavity in the skull, then continuing further towards the interior with comparative independence. The eye itself, although permeated with life, is remarkably like a physical apparatus. The processes in the eye and the processes in a physical apparatus can be characterized in a remarkably similar way. The soul, it is true, comprises the processes arising in the eye, but, as I have often said, the sense-organs or the spheres of the senses are like gulfs which the outer world extends into us, as it were, and in the spheres of the senses we participate far more in the outer world than we do in the other domains of our organism.

When we turn our attention to some inner organ such as the kidneys, for example, we cannot say that there we share in something external by virtue of experiencing the processes of the organ itself. But in experiencing what goes on in the senses, we experience the outer world at the same time. I beg you to disregard entirely things that may be known to you from treatises on the physiology of the senses and so forth. I am not now referring to any of these things but to the fact that is perfectly accessible to ordinary human understanding, namely, that the process which takes place in the senses can more readily be grasped as something that extends into us from without and in which we participate, than as something we bring about inwardly through our organism. Hence it is also a fact that in the senses our astral body is practically in the outer world. Especially when we have deliberately surrendered ourselves to sense-perceptions of the outer world, our astral body is actually almost entirely submerged in the outer world, though not to the same extent in the case of all the senses. It is *completely* submerged in the outer world while we sleep. So that from this point of view sleep is a kind of enhancement of surrender of the senses to the outer world. When your eyes are closed, your astral body also withdraws more into the interior of the head; it belongs more to you yourself. When you look out in the normal way, then the astral body draws into the eye and participates in the outer world. If it passes entirely out of your organism, then you go to sleep. Surrender of the senses to the outer world is, in fact, not what is ordinarily supposed, but as regards consciousness is really a stage on the way to going to sleep.

Thus in acts of sense-perception man participates to some extent in the outer world; in sleep he participates in it fully. With Inspiration (knowledge through Inspiration) he can become aware of what is going on in the world in which he is with his astral body between sleeping and waking.

With Inspired Cognition, however, man can become aware of something else, namely the moment of waking. The moment of waking is as it were something that is more intense, more vivid, but may nevertheless be compared with closing the eyes.

When I am standing in front of a color, I surrender my astral body to that in the eye which, as I said, is nearly outside, namely, the process occasioned by a color from the external world making an impression upon my eye. When I close my eyes I draw my astral body back into myself; when I wake, I draw my astral body back from the outer world, from the Cosmos. Often, infinitely often during the waking life of day, in connection with the eyes or the ears, for example, I do the same with my astral body as I do on waking, only then my whole organism is involved as a totality. On waking I draw back my whole astral body. Naturally, this process of drawing back the astral body on waking remains unconscious in the ordinary way, just as the sense-process itself remains unconscious. But if this moment of waking becomes a conscious experience for one who has reached the stage of Inspiration, it is at once evident that this entrance of the astral body takes place in a quite different world from that in which we otherwise live; above all it is very often obvious how difficult it is for the astral body to come back again into the physical and etheric bodies. Hindrances are there.

It can truly be said that one who begins to be aware of this process of the return of the astral body into the physical and etheric bodies experiences spiritual storms and percussions. These spiritual storms show that the astral body is diving down into the physical and etheric bodies but these bodies are not like the descriptions given by anatomists and physiologists, for they too belong to a *spiritual* world. Both the so-called physical body and the somewhat nebulous etheric body are rooted in a spiritual world. In its real nature the physical body reveals itself as something quite different from the material image presented to the eye or to ordinary science.

This descent of the astral body into the physical and etheric bodies can appear in imagery of infinite variety. Let us say a burning piece of wood drops spluttering into water—that is the simplest, the most abstract analogy for the experience that may arise in one who is just beginning to have knowledge of this process. But then it becomes inwardly real in manifold ways, and is afterwards completely spiritualized inasmuch as what at first can only be compared in its appearance to a raging storm becomes permeated subsequently with harmonious movements, giving the impression that something is speaking, is saying or announcing something.

What is thus announced clothes itself to begin with in pictures of reminiscences from ordinary life; but this changes

103

in course of time and we gradually come to experience a world that is also around us but in which our experiences cannot be called reminiscences of ordinary perceptions, because they are of an entirely different character and because they show us in themselves that this is a different world. It can be perceived that man with his astral body passes out of his environment into the physical and etheric bodies by way of the whole breathing process. The astral body that is active in the senses contacts the delicate ramifications of the breathing process and penetrates into the subtle rhythms in which the breathing process reaches into the sphere of the senses. At the moment of waking the astral body leaves the outer world, enters into the physical and etheric bodies and seizes hold of the breathing process which has been left to itself during the period of sleep. Along the paths of the breathing processes, of the moving breath, the astral body enters into the physical and etheric bodies and spreads out as does the breath itself.

At the moment of waking, ordinary consciousness swiftly obtrudes itself into the perception of the outer world, and quickly unites experience of the breathing process with experience of the organism as a whole. Consciousness at the stage of Inspiration can separate this flow of the astral body along the paths of the breathing rhythm and become aware of the rest of the organic process—although naturally the latter does not take its course on its own. Not only at this moment of waking, but at every moment the movement of the breath in the human organism is of course connected inwardly with the other processes in the organism. But in the higher consciousness of Inspiration the two can be separated. We follow how the astral body, moving along the paths of the rhythmical breathing, enters into the physical body, and then we learn to know something that otherwise remains completely unconscious.

After having experienced all the states of consciousness which accompany this entrance of the astral body and are objective—not subjective—states of feeling, the knowledge comes to us that man, inasmuch as he is not merely a being of sense but also a being of breath, has his roots in the world I have called in *Occult Science* the world of the Archangeloi. Just as the Beings of the supersensible world standing one stage above man are active in his sense-processes, so are the Beings of the spiritual world standing two stages above him active in his breathing process. They pass in and out, as it were, as he goes to sleep and wakes.

Something of great significance for human life presents itself to us when we observe these processes. If our waking life was not interrupted by sleep, although impressions of the outer world would come to us, these impressions would last only for a short time. We could not develop a lasting power of memory. You know how fleetingly the pictures work in the senses as after-images. Processes activated more deeply in the organism continue to work for a longer time; but the after-effects would not continue for more than a few days if we did not sleep.

What is it that actually goes on in sleep? Here I must remind you of something I said here very recently, describing how during sleep, with his astral body and his ego, man always lives through in backward order what he has experienced in the physical world in the preceding waking period. Let us take a regular waking period and a regular sleeping period—it is however just the same for irregular periods. A man wakes up on a certain morning, busies himself during the day, goes to rest in the evening and sleeps through the night for about a third of the time he has been awake. Between waking and going to sleep he has a series of experiences, daytime experiences. During sleep he actually lives through in backward order what had been experienced during the day. The life of sleep goes backward with greater rapidity, so that only a third of the time is needed.

What has actually happened? If we were to sleep according to the laws of the physical world—I do not now mean the body, for the body sleeps according to those laws as a matter of course—but if in the conditions of existence outside the physical and etheric bodies, in our ego and our astral body, our sleep were governed by the same laws which govern our waking life by day, this movement backwards would not be possible, for we should simply have to go forward with the flow of time. We are subject to altogether different laws when in our astral body and ego we are outside the physical and etheric bodies.

Now think of the following. Today is the 22nd December; this morning was for you, when you woke from sleep, the morning of the 22nd December. Presently you will go to sleep and by the time you wake tomorrow, your experiences in their backward order, will have brought you again to the morning of today, the 22nd December. So you have gone through an inner process in which you have turned back. When you wake tomorrow, the morning of 23rd December, the process will have carried you back to the morning of the 22nd December. You wake up; at the same moment—because now your astral body, contrary to the laws it has been obeying during your sleep, makes the jerk through your body into the ordinary physical world—at the same moment you are compelled in your inmost soul-life to go forward quickly with your ego and astral body to the morning of the 23rd December. You actually pass through this process inwardly.

106

I want you to grasp in its full significance what I am now going to say. If you have some kind of gas in a closed vessel, you can compress this gas so that it becomes denser. That is a process in Space. But it can be compared—naturally *only* compared—with what I have just been describing to you. You go back in your astral body and your ego to the morning of December 22nd, and then, when you next wake, you jerk quickly forward to the morning of December 23rd. You impel your soul forward in *Time*. And through this process your soul-being, your astral body, becomes so condensed within Time, that it carries the impressions of the outer world not only for a short period, but as enduring memory. Just as any gas that is condensed exercises a stronger pressure, has more inner power, so does your astral body acquire the strong power of remembrance, of memory, through this inner condensation in Time.

This gives us an idea of something that otherwise always escapes our consciousness. We are apt to conceive that Time flows on evenly, and that everything taking place in Time also flows on evenly with it. As regards Space we know that whatever is extended in Space can be condensed; its inner power of expansion increases. But what lives in Time, the element of soul, can be condensed too—I am speaking figuratively, of course—and then its inner power increases. And for man, one of these powers is the power of memory.

We actually owe this power of remembrance, of memory, to what happens during our sleep. From the time of going to sleep until waking we are in the world of the Archangeloi, and together with the Beings of that hierarchy we cultivate this power of memory. Just as we cultivate the power of sense-perception and the combining of sense-perceptions together with the Beings of the hierarchy of the Angeloi, so do we cultivate this power of memory, which is a more in-

107

ward power, more connected with the centre of our being, in communion with the world of the Archangeloi.

True knowledge of man does not exist in a nebulous, mystic form of brooding introspection; true knowledge of man, with every further step that is taken into the inner life, leads at the same time into higher worlds. We have spoken today of two such steps. If we contemplate the sphere of the senses we are in the sphere of the Angeloi; if we contemplate the sphere of memory, we are in the sphere of the Archangloi. Self-knowledge is at the same time knowledge of the Gods, knowledge of Spirit, because every step that leads into man's inner being leads *ipso facto* into the spiritual world. And the deeper the penetration within, the higher—to use a paradox—is the ascent into the world of spiritual Beings. Self-knowledge, if it is earnest, is true World-knowledge, namely, knowledge of the spiritual content of the World.

From what has been said you can understand why in ancient times, when certain oriental peoples were striving to acquire an instinctive kind of spiritual vision, the aim was to make the breathing process into a conscious process by means of special breathing exercises. In point of fact, as soon as the breathing process becomes a conscious process, we enter into a spiritual world.

I need not say again today that those ancient practices should not be repeated by modern man with his different constitution, but should be replaced by others which are set forth in the books mentioned. It can however be said with truth in the case of both kinds of knowledge, the knowledge based upon the old, mystical clairvoyance and the knowledge yielded by the exact clairvoyance proper to the modern age, that genuine observation of the processes which take place inwardly in man leads at the same time into the spiritual world.

There are people who say: All this is unspiritual, for the

aim is to investigate the senses, the breathing. They call it materialistic self-knowledge in comparison with nebulous mystical experience. But let them try to practice it for once! They will soon discover that genuine knowledge of the sense-process reveals it to be a spiritual process and that to regard it as a material process is sheer illusion. And the same applies to the breathing process. The breathing process is a material process only when seen externally. Seen from within, it is through and through a spiritual process, actually taking its course in a world far higher than the world we perceive through our senses.

THE SPIRITUAL COMMUNION
OF MANKIND

I

Midsummer and Midwinter Mysteries.

T HE Christmas festival can be the occasion for com- Dornach, December 23, 1922
paring the Mystery upon which it is based with Mysteries
that were the outcome of different conditions in the evolution of humanity. The Christmas Mystery—when it is conceived as a Mystery—belongs paramountly to *Winter.* It
arose from conceptions of the spiritual world that had primarily to do with the link established between man and the
scene of his life on Earth at the beginning of Winter.

When we turn our attention to Mysteries that were celebrated in certain parts of Asia long before the founding of
Christianity and in which many sublime cosmic thoughts
were given expression, or when we compare the Christmas
festival with Mysteries that were celebrated also in pre-
Christian times, in Middle, Northern and Western Europe,
we are struck by the fact that they were preeminently *Summer* Mysteries, connected with the union between man and
all that takes place in earthly life during the time of Summer.
To understand the essential meaning of these Mysteries we

110

must think, first of all, of that part of the evolution of humanity which preceded the Mystery of Golgotha.

Looking back into very ancient times we find that the Mysteries were institutions of men still possessed of the faculty of instinctive clairvoyance. In certain states of consciousness between those of full sleep and waking, in states where dreams were expressions of reality, the men belonging to that ancient humanity were still able to gaze into the spiritual worlds whence the human being descends into his physical body on the Earth. Every human being in those times could speak and think about the spiritual worlds, just as a man today can speak about the ordinary knowledge he has learnt at school. I have, as you know, often said that what the men of those olden times beheld of the spiritual-supersensible world presented itself to them in *pictures*—not the pictures of dreams but somewhat resembling them. Whereas we know quite well that the pictures in our dreams are woven from our reminiscences, that they rise up from the organism and, unlike our thoughts, do not mirror reality, through the very nature of the Imaginations of the old clairvoyance men knew that they were the expressions—not, it is true, of any external, material reality nor of any historical reality, but of a spiritual world lying hidden behind the physical world. Thus the spiritual world was revealed to men in *pictures*.

But it must not be imagined that those men of an earlier epoch had no thoughts. They *had* thoughts, but they did not acquire them as man acquires his thoughts today. If a man of the modern age is to have thoughts, he must exert himself inwardly; he must elaborate his thoughts by dint of inner effort. A similar kind of activity was, it is true, exercised by the men of old in connection with the pictures which

111

mirrored for them a spiritual form of existence; but the thoughts came with the pictures. One may well be amazed at the power and brilliance of the thoughts of that old humanity; but the thoughts were not formulated by dint of effort; they were received as revelations.

Now just as we today have schools and colleges, so in those times there were Mysteries—institutions in which science, art and religion were undivided. No distinction was made between belief and knowledge. Knowledge came in the form of pictures; but belief was based securely on knowledge. Nor was any distinction made between what men fashioned out of various materials into works of art, and what they acquired as wisdom. Today the distinction is made by saying: What man acquires in the form of wisdom must be *true;* but what he embodies in his materials as a painter, sculptor or musician—that is fantasy!

Goethe was really the last survivor of those who did *not* hold this view. He regarded as truth both what he embodied in his materials as an artist and what he took to be science. The philistinism expressed in the distinction between the artistic and the scientific did not, in fact, appear until comparatively late, indeed after Goethe's time. Goethe was still able, when he saw the works of art in Italy, to utter the beautiful words: "I have the idea that in the creation of their works of art the Greeks proceeded by the same laws by which Nature herself creates and of which I am on the track." In Weimar, before going to Italy, he and Herder had studied the philosophy of Spinoza together. Goethe had striven to deepen his realization that all the beings in man's environment are permeated by the divine-spiritual. He also tried to discover the manifestations of this divine-spiritual in details, for example in the leaf and flower of the plant. And the way in which he built up for himself a picture of the plant-

112

form and animal-form in his botanical and zoological studies was identical as an activity of soul with the procedure he adopted in his artistic creations.

Today it is considered unscientific to speak of one and the same truth in art, in science and in religion. But as I have said, in those ancient centres of learning and culture, art, science and religion were one. It was actually the leaders in these Mysteries who began gradually to separate out particular thoughts from those that were revealed to men with their instinctive clairvoyance and to establish a wisdom composed of thoughts. On all sides we see a wisdom composed of thoughts emerging in the Mysteries from clairvoyant vision. Whereas the majority of men were content with pictorial vision, were satisfied to have the revelation of this spiritual vision presented to them in the form of myths, fairy-tales and legends by those who were capable of doing so, the leaders of the Mysteries were working at the development of a wisdom composed of thoughts. But they were fully aware that this wisdom was *revealed,* not acquired by man's own powers.

We must try to transport ourselves into this quite different attitude of soul. I will put it in the following way.—When the man of today conceives a thought, he ascribes it to his own activity of thinking. He forms chains of thoughts in accordance with rules of logic—which are themselves the product of his own thinking. The man of olden times *received* the thoughts. He paid no heed at all to how the connections between thoughts should be formulated, for they came to him as revelations. But this meant that he did not live in his thoughts in the way we live in ours We regard our thoughts as the possession of our soul; we know that we have worked to acquire them. They have, as it were, been born from our own life of soul, they have arisen out of ourselves, and we regard them as our property. The man of olden time could not regard his thoughts in this way. They were illuminations; they had come to him together with the pictures. And this gave rise to a very definite feeling and attitude towards the wisdom-filled thoughts. Man said to himself as he contemplated his thoughts: "A divine Being from a higher world has descended into me. I partake of the thoughts which in reality *other Beings* are thinking—Beings who are higher than man but who inspire me, who live in me, who give me these thoughts. I can therefore only regard the thoughts as having been vouchsafed to me by Grace from above." It was because the man of old held this view that he felt the need at certain seasons to make an offering of these thoughts to the higher Beings, as it were through his feelings. And this was done in the Summer Mysteries.

In the Summer the Earth is more given up to its own environment, to the atmosphere surrounding it. It has not contracted because of the cold or enveloped itself in a raiment of snow; it is in perpetual intercourse with its atmospheric environment. Hence man too is given up to the wide cosmic expanse. In the Summer he feels himself united with the Upper Gods. And in those ancient times man waited for the Midsummer season—the time when the Sun is at the zenith of its power—in order at this season and in certain places he regarded as sacred, to establish contact with the Upper Gods. He availed himself of his natural connection in Summer with the whole etheric environment, in order out of his deepest feelings to make a sacrificial offering to the Gods who had revealed their thoughts to him.

The teachers in the Mysteries spoke to their pupils somewhat as follows. They said: "Every year at Midsummer, a solemn offering must be made to the Upper Gods in gratitude for the thoughts they vouchsafe to man. For if this is not

114

done it is all too easy for the Luciferic powers to invade man's thinking and he is then permeated by these powers. He can avoid this if every Summer he is mindful of how the Upper Gods have given him these thoughts and at the Midsummer season lets his thoughts flow back again, as it were, to the Gods." In this way the men of olden times tried to safeguard themselves from Luciferic influences. The leaders of the Mysteries called together those who were in a sense their pupils and in their presence enacted that solemn rite at the culmination of which the thoughts that had been revealed by the Upper Gods were now offered up to them in upward-streaming feelings.

The external rite consisted in solemn words being spoken into rising smoke which was thus set into waves. This act was merely meant to signify that the offering made by man's inmost soul to the Upper Gods was being inscribed into an outer medium—the rising smoke—through form-creating words. The words of the prayer inscribed into the rising smoke the feelings which the soul desired to send upwards to the Gods as an offering for the thoughts they had revealed.

This was the basic mood of soul underlying the celebration of the Midsummer Mysteries. These Midsummer festivals had meaning only as long as men received their thoughts by way of revelation.

But in the centuries immediately preceding the Mystery of Golgotha—beginning as early as the 8th and 9th centuries B.C.—these thoughts that were revealed from above grew dark, and more and more there awakened in man the faculty to acquire his thoughts through his own efforts. This induced in him an entirely different mood. Whereas formerly he had felt that his thoughts were coming to him as it were from the far spaces of the universe, descending into his inner life, he now began to feel the thoughts as something unfolding within himself, belonging to him like the blood in his veins. In olden times, thoughts had been regarded more as something belonging to man like the *breath*—the breath that is received from the surrounding atmosphere and continually given back again. Just as man regards the air as something which surrounds him, which he draws into himself but always gives out again, so did he feel his thoughts as something which he did not draw into himself but which was received by him through revelation and must ever and again be given back to the Gods at the time of Midsummer.

The festivals themselves were given a dramatic form in keeping with this attitude. The leaders of the Mysteries went to the ceremonies bearing the symbols of wisdom; and as they conducted the sacrificial rites they divested themselves of the symbols one by one. Then, when they went away from the ceremonies, having laid aside the symbols of wisdom, they appeared as men who must acquire their wisdom again in the course of the year. It was like a confession on the part of those sages of olden times. When they had made the solemn offering it was as though they declared to the masses of those who were their followers: "We have become nescient again."

To share in this way in the course taken by the seasons of the year, entering as Midsummer approaches into the possession of wisdom, then passing into a state of nescience (*Torheit*) before becoming wise again—this was actually felt by men to be a means of escape from the Luciferic powers. They strove to participate in the life of the cosmos. As the cosmos lets Winter alternate with Summer, so did they let the time of wisdom alternate in themselves with the time of entry into the darkness of ignorance.

Now there were some whose wisdom was needed all the year round, and who for this reason could not act or adopt the same procedure as the others. For example, there were teachers in the Mysteries who practised the art of healing—for that too was part of the Mysteries. Naturally it would not do for a doctor to become ignorant in August and September—if I may use the present names of the months—so these men were allowed to retain their wisdom, but in return they made the sacrifice of being only servants in the Mysteries. Those who were the leaders became ignorant for a certain time every year.

Reminiscences of this have remained here and there, for example in the figure described by Goethe in his poem *Die Geheimnisse* as the 'Thirteenth,' the one who was the leader of the others but was himself in a state of dullness rather than wisdom.

All these things are evidence that the attitude towards the guiding wisdom of mankind was entirely different from what it afterwards became when men began to regard their thoughts as produced by themselves. Whereas formerly man felt that wisdom was like the air he breathes, later on he felt that his thoughts were produced within himself, like the blood. We can therefore say: In ancient times man felt his thoughts to be like the air of the breath and in the epoch of the Mystery of Golgotha he began to feel that they were like the blood within him.

But then man also said to himself: "What I experience as thought is now no longer heavenly, it is no longer something that has descended from above. It is something that arises in the human being himself, something that is earthly."—This feeling that the thoughts of men are earthly in origin was still significantly present at the time of the Mystery of Golgotha among those who were the late successors of the leaders of the ancient Mysteries. Those who stood at that time at the height of cultural life said to themselves: Man

117

can no longer have such thoughts as had the sages of old, who with their thoughts lived together with the Gods; he must now develop purely human thoughts. But these purely human thoughts are in danger of falling prey to the Ahrimanic powers. The thoughts that were revealed to man from above were in danger of succumbing to the Luciferic powers; the human thoughts, the self-produced thoughts, are in danger of succumbing to the Ahrimanic powers.

Those who were capable of thinking in this way in the epoch of the Mystery of Golgotha—by the 4th century, however, the insight was lost—such men experienced the Mystery of Golgotha as the true redemption of mankind. They said to themselves: The spiritual Power indwelling the Sun could hitherto be attained only by superhuman forces. This Power must now be attained by human faculties, for man's thoughts are now within his own being. Hence he must inwardly raise these thoughts of his to the Divine. Now that he is an earthly thinker, he must permeate his thoughts inwardly with the Divine, and this he can do through uniting himself in thought and feeling with the Mystery of Golgotha.

This meant that the festival once celebrated in the Mysteries at Midsummer became a *Winter* festival. In Winter, when the earth envelops herself in her raiment of snow and is no longer in living interchange with the atmosphere around her, man too is fettered more strongly to the earth; he does not share in the life of the wide universe but enters into the life that is rooted beneath the soil of the earth.—But the meaning of this must be understood.

We can continually be made aware of how in the earth's environment there is not only that which comes directly from the Sun but also that which partakes in the life of the earth beneath the surface of the soil. I have spoken of this before by referring to some very simple facts.—Those of you who have lived in the country will know how the peasants dig pits in the earth during Winter and put their potatoes in them. Down there in the earth the potatoes last splendidly through the Winter, which would not be the case if they were simply put in cellars. Why is this?—Think of an area of the earth's surface. It absorbs the light and warmth of the Sun that have streamed to it during the Summer. The light and the warmth sink down, as it were, into the soil of the earth, so that in Winter the Summer is still there, under the soil. During Winter it is Summer underneath the surface of the earth. And it is this Summer under the surface of the earth in Winter time that enables the roots of the plants to thrive. The seeds become roots and growth begins. So when we see a plant growing this year it is actually being enabled to grow by the forces of *last* year's Sun which had penetrated into the earth.

When therefore we are looking at the root of a plant, or even at parts of the leaves, we have before us what is the *previous Summer* in the plant. It is only in the blossom that we have *this* year's Summer, for the blossom is conjured forth by the light and warmth of the present year's Sun. In the sprouting and unfolding of the plant we still have the previous year and the present year comes to manifestation only in the blossom. Even the ovary at the centre of the blossom is a product of the Winter—in reality, that is, of the previous Summer. Only what *surrounds* the ovary belongs to the present year. Thus do the seasons interpenetrate. When the earth dons her Winter raiment of snow, beneath that raiment is the continuation of Summer. Man does not now unite himself with the wide expanse but turns his life of soul inwards, into the interior of the earth. He turns to the Lower Gods.

This was the conception held by men who were in posses-

119

sion of the heritage of the ancient wisdom at the time of the Mystery of Golgotha. And it was this that made them realize: It is in what is united with the earth that we must seek the power of the Christ, the power of the new wisdom which permeates the future evolution of the earth. Having passed to the stage of self-produced thoughts, man felt the need to unite these thoughts inwardly with the Divine, to permeate them inwardly with the Divine, in other words, with the Christ Impulse. This he can do at the time when he is most closely bound to the earth—in deep Winter; he can do it when the earth shuts herself off from the cosmos. For then he too is shut off from the cosmos and comes nearest to the God who descended from those far spaces and united Himself with the earth.

It is a beautiful thought to connect the Christmas festival with the time when the earth is shut off from the cosmos, when in the loneliness of earth man seeks to establish for his self-produced thoughts communion with divine-spiritual-supersensible reality, and when, understanding what this means, he endeavors to protect himself from the Ahrimanic powers, as in ancient times he protected himself from the Luciferic powers through the rites of the Midsummer Mysteries.

And as under the guidance of the teachers in the Mysteries the man of olden time became aware through the Midsummer festival that his thoughts were fading into a state of twilight, the man of today who rightly understands the Christmas Mystery should feel strengthened when at Christmas he steeps himself in truths such as have now once more been expressed. He should feel how through developing a true relation to the Mystery of Golgotha, the thoughts he acquires in the darkness of his inner life can be illumined. For it is indeed so when he realizes that once in the course of the

120

earth's evolution the Being who in pre-Christian ages could only be thought of as united with the Sun, passed into earthly evolution and together with mankind indwells the earth as a Spiritual Being. In contrast to the old Midsummer festivals where the aim was that a man should pass out of himself into the cosmos, the Christmas festival should be the occasion when man tries to deepen inwardly, to spiritualize, whatever knowledge he acquires about the great world.

The man of old did not feel that knowledge was his own possession but that it was a gift bestowed upon him, and every year he gave it back again. The man of today necessarily regards his world of thought, his intellectual knowledge, as his own possession. Therefore he must receive into his heart the Spirit Being who has united with the Earth; he must link his thoughts with this Being in order that instead of remaining with his thoughts in egotistic seclusion, he shall unite these thoughts of his with that Being of Sun and Earth who fulfilled the Mystery of Golgotha.

In a certain respect the ancient Mysteries had what might be called an 'aristocratic' character. Indeed the principle of aristocracy really had its origin in those old Mysteries, for it was the priests who enacted the sacrifice on behalf of all the others.

The Christmas festival has a 'democratic' character. What modern men acquire as that which really makes them man, is their inner store of thoughts. And the Christmas Mystery is only truly celebrated when the one does not make the sacrificial offering for another, but when the one shares with the other a common experience: equality in face of the Sun Being who came down to the Earth. And in the early period of Christian evolution—until about the 4th century—it was this that was felt to be a particularly significant principle of Christianity. It was not until then that the old forms of the

Egyptian Mysteries were resuscitated and made their way via Rome to Western Europe, overlaying the original Christianity and shrouding it in traditions which will have to be superseded if Christianity is to be rightly understood. For the character with which Christianity was invested by Rome was essentially that of the old Mysteries. In accordance with *true* Christianity, this finding of the spiritual-supersensible reality in man must take place at a time *not* when he passes out of himself and is given up to the Cosmos, but when he is firmly *within* himself. And this is most of all the case when he is united with the Earth at the time when the Earth herself is shut off from the cosmic expanse—that is to say, in Midwinter.

I have thus tried to show how it came about that in the course of the ages the Midsummer festivals in the Mysteries changed into the Midwinter Christmas Mystery. But this must be understood in the right sense. By looking back over the evolution of humanity we can deepen our understanding of what is presented to us in the Christmas Mystery. By contrasting it with olden times we can feel the importance of the fact that man has now to look *within himself* for the secrets he once sought to find outside his own being.

It is from this point of view that my *Occult Science* is written. If such a book had been written in ancient times (then, of course, it would not have been a book but something different!) the starting-point of the descriptions would have been the starry heavens. But in the book as it is, the starting-point is *man:* contemplation, first of the inner aspect of man's being and proceeding from there to the universe. The inner core of man's being is traced through the epochs of Old Saturn, Old Sun, Old Moon, and extended to the future epochs of the Earth's evolution.

In seeking for knowledge of the world in ancient times,

men started by contemplating the stars; then they endeavored to apply to the inner constitution of the human being what they learned from the stars. For example, they contemplated the Sun which revealed a very great deal to the Imaginative cognition of those days. To the orthodox modern scientist the Sun is a ball of gas—which of course it cannot be for unbiased thought. When the man of ancient time contemplated the Sun externally, it was to him the bodily expression of soul-and-spirit, just as the human body is an expression of soul-and-spirit. Very much was learnt from the Sun. And when man had read in the Cosmos what the Sun had revealed to him, he could point to his own heart, and say: Now I understand the nature of the human heart, for the Sun has revealed it to me!—And similarly in the other heavenly bodies and constellations, man discovered the secrets of his organism.

It was not possible to proceed in this way in the book *Occult Science*. Although it is too soon yet for all the relevant details to have been worked out, the procedure is that we think, first, of the human being as a whole, with heart, lungs, and so on, and in understanding the organs individually we come to understand the universe. We study the human heart, for example, and what we read there tells us what the Sun is, tells us something about the nature of the Sun. Thus through the heart we learn to know the nature of the Sun; that is to say, we proceed from within outwards. In ancient times it was the other way about: first of all men learnt to know the nature of the Sun and then they understood the nature of the human heart. In the modern age we learn what the heart is, what the lung is . . . and so, starting from man, we learn to know the universe.

The ancients could only give expression to their awareness of this relation of man to the universe by looking upwards to the Sun and the starry heavens at the time of Midsummer, when conditions were the most favorable for feeling their union with the Cosmos. But if we today would realize with inner intensity how we can come to know the universe, we must gaze into the depths of man's inner being. And the right time for this is in Midwinter, at Christmas.

Try to grasp the full meaning of this Christmas thought, my dear friends, for there is a real need today to give life again to old habits such as these. We need, for example, to be sincere again in our experience of the course of the year. All that numbers of people know today about Christmas is that it is a time for giving presents, also—perhaps, a time when in a very external way, thought is turned to the Mystery of Golgotha!

It is superficialities such as these that are really to blame for the great calamity into which human civilization has drifted today. It is there that much of the real blame must be placed; it lies in the clinging to habits, and in the unwillingness to realize the necessity of *renewal*—the need, for example, to imbue the true Christmas thought, the true Christmas feeling, with new life.

This impulse of renewal is needed because we can only become Man again in the true sense by finding the spiritual part of our being. It is a 'World-Christmas' that we need, a birth of spiritual life. Then we shall once again celebrate Christmas as honest human beings; again there will be meaning in the fact that at the time when the Earth is shrouded in her raiment of snow, we try to feel that our world of thought is permeated with the Christ Impulse—the world of thought which today is like the blood within us, in contrast to the old world of thought which was like the breath.

We must learn to live more intensely with the course of the seasons than is the custom today. About 20 years ago the idea occurred that it would be advantageous to have a fixed Easter—a festival which is still regulated by the actual course of time. The idea was that Easter should be fixed permanently at the beginning of April, so that account books might not always be thrown into confusion owing to the dates of the festival varying each year. Even man's experience of the flow of time was to be drawn into the materialistic trend of evolution. In view of other things that have happened as well, it would not be surprising if materialistic thought were ultimately to accept this arrangement. For example, men begin the year with the present New Year's Day, the 1st of January, in spite of the fact that December (decem) is the tenth month, and January and February quite obviously belong to the previous year; so that in reality the new year can begin in March at the earliest—as indeed was actually the case in Roman times. But it once pleased a French King (whom even history acknowledges to have been an imbecile) to begin the year in the middle of the Winter, on the 1st of January, and humanity has followed suit.

Strong and resolute thoughts are needed to admit honestly to ourselves that the saving of human evolution depends upon man allying himself with *wisdom*. Many things indicate that he has by no means always done so but has very often allied himself with ignorance, with nescience. The Christmas thought must be taken sincerely and honestly, in connection with the Being who said: "I am the Way, the Truth, and the Life." But the way to the Truth and to the Life in the Spirit has to be deliberately sought, and for this it is necessary for modern humanity to plunge down into the dark depths of midnight in order to find the light that kindles itself in man.

The old tradition of the first Christmas Mass being read at midnight is not enough. Man must again realize in actual

125

experience that what is best and most filled with light in his nature is born out of the darkness prevailing in himself. *The true light is born out of the darkness.* And from this darkness *light* must be born—not further darkness.

Try to permeate the Christmas thought with the strength that will come to your souls when you feel with all intensity that the light of spiritual insight and spiritual vision must pierce the darkness of knowledge of another kind. Then in the Holy Night, Christ will be born in the heart of each one of you, and you will experience together with all mankind, a World-Christmas.

II

The Mysteries of Man's Nature and the
Course of the Year.

Dornach, December 24, 1922

IF we would deepen our thoughts at this time in a manner suitable for the present age, this will best be done in the way indicated yesterday, namely, by looking back over the process of human evolution in order to recognize from the spiritual guidance vouchsafed to mankind hitherto, what tasks devolve upon men today. It must not, of course, be forgotten that the point of salient importance in the Christmas thought is that in the night just beginning the Light of Christ shone into the evolution of humanity at the point of time when through this Event, through this integration, as it were, of the Mystery of Golgotha into earthly life, *meaning* was given to man's life on Earth, and therewith to the Earth herself.

Yesterday I spoke to you of how in the times before the Mystery of Golgotha an important rôle was played by the festivals that were celebrated in the Mysteries at Midsummer, when man, together with the Earth, opens his being to the Cosmos and when his soul can enter into union with Powers belonging to realms beyond the Earth. We heard how among certain peoples the leaders of the Mysteries, following the path along which, at Midsummer, at our St. John's tide, the human soul can be led into the divine-spiritual worlds, offered up their thoughts and feelings to the divine-spiritual Powers. They did this because they realized that whatever revealed itself to them in the course of the year was exposed to the temptations of the Luciferic powers unless at Midsummer, when the Earth spreads wide her wings into the cosmic expanse, these thoughts were felt to be Grace bestowed by the divine-spiritual Beings.

I went on to show how the evolutionary process brought it about that for a certain section of mankind, the Midwinter festival quite naturally replaced the Midsummer festival. Even in our present vapid Christmas thoughts something is still left of this Midwinter festival. The birth of the Saviour in the Midwinter night is either celebrated in religious communities, or, because a man feels that he must again find the way to the light of the Spirit, he celebrates Christmas in the stillness of his own heart, conscious that at this time of the year he is closest to the Earth and her life when he is alone with himself. For the Earth too, at this time, is shut off from the Cosmos; enveloped in her raiment of snow she lives in cosmic space as a being indrawn and isolated.

Christmas thoughts played a part even in the times when among certain peoples the Midsummer festival was still of paramount importance, but in the pre-Christian era the meaning of the Christmas thought was not the same as it is today. At that time the sublime Sun Spirit still belonged to the Cosmos, had not yet come down to the Earth. The whole condition of the human soul at Midwinter, when together with the Earth man felt himself to be in a kind of cosmic isolation, was different from what it is today. And we learn to know what this condition was if we turn our attention to certain Mysteries that were celebrated mainly in the South in times long, long before the Mystery of Golgotha. Initiation in those Mysteries was conferred upon candidates in the old way, the Initiation-Science of that day was imparted to them. And among certain ancient peoples this Initiation-Science consisted in the candidate learning

128

to read the Book of the World—I do not mean anything that is conveyed by dead letters written on paper, but what the Beings of the universe themselves communicate. Those who have insight into the secrets of the Cosmos know that everything growing and thriving on the Earth is an image of what shines down from the stars out of the cosmic expanse.

A man who learnt this cosmic reading as we today learn the far simpler kind of reading by means of dead letters, knew that he must see in every plant a sign revealing to him something of the secrets of the Universe, and that when he let his gaze survey the world of plants or animals, this survey was itself a form of reading. And it was in such a way that the Initiates of certain ancient Mysteries taught their pupils. They did not read to them out of a book but communicated to them what they experienced under the inspiration of the so-called Year-God concerning the secrets of the course of the year and their significance for human life.

It was in this way that an ancient wisdom related world-beings and world-happenings to what concerned the life of man. When the sages of old communicated such things to their pupils, they were inspired by divine-spiritual Beings such as the Year-God.

Who was this Year-God who belonged to the rank of the Primal Powers, or Archai, in the Hierarchies? Who was this Year-God? He was a Being to whom certain of those who were versed in Initiation-Science lifted their hearts and in so doing were endowed by him with the power and inner light enabling them to read one thing from the budding plants in Spring, another from the ripening of the early fruits in Summer, another when the leaves redden in Autumn and the fruits ripen, and yet another when the trees glitter under the snowflakes and the Earth with her rocks is covered with a veil of snow. This 'reading' lasted for a whole year—

through Spring, Summer, Autumn and Winter; and in this reading the secrets of Man himself were unveiled in the intercourse between teachers and pupils. And then the cycle of the year began anew.

Some idea of what these ancient Initiates taught to their pupils under the inspiration of the Year-God may be conveyed in the following way. The attention of the pupils was drawn, first of all, to what is revealed in Spring, when the snow is over and the Sun is gaining strength, when the first buds of the plants are appearing and the forces of the Earth are being renewed. The pupils were made aware of how a plant growing in the meadows and a plant growing in the shade of the trees in a forest, speak differently of the secrets of the universe. They were made aware of how in the various plants the warmth and light of the Sun speak differently from the cosmic expanse in the round or serrated leaves.

And what could be revealed in this way under the influence and inspiration of the Year-God through the the letters budding forth from the Earth herself, unveiled to the pupils of the teachers in the Mysteries, in the manner of that time, secrets of the physical body of man.

The teachers pointed to the physical productiveness of the Earth, to the force of the Earth shooting into the plant. At every single place on the Earth to which the pupil's attention was directed, there was a different 'letter.' These letters —which were living plant-beings, or living animal forms— were then combined as we today combine single letters into words. In sharing thus in the life of Spring, man was reading in Nature. The Initiations bestowed by the Year-God consisted in this reading. And when Spring came to an end, at about the time of the month of May, man had the impression: Now I understand how out of the womb of the universe the human physical body takes shape and is formed.

Then came the Summer. The same letters and words of the great cosmic Logos were used, but it was pointed out to the pupils how under the Sun's rays which stream differently now, under its light and warmth which now work in a different way, the letters change their forms, how the first buds, which had spoken of the secrets of the human physical body, open themselves to the Sun in the blossoms. These many-colored blossoms were now letters used by the pupil; each blossom made him feel how the Sun's ray lovingly kisses the plant-forces springing up from the Earth. And in the wonderfully delicate and tender process of the cosmic forces weaving over the Earth-forces in the blossoming plants, he read the words which conveyed to him how the Earth strives outwards into the cosmic expanse. Man lived in union with the Earth as she opened herself to the Cosmos, to the distant stars, lived with the Earth herself in the infinitudes.

What lay hidden in these infinitudes revealed itself to man as he gazed at the letters which were the blossoming plants. He read out of these letters what the conditions of life had been for the human being who has descended from the spiritual worlds to physical existence on the Earth; how he had gathered together etheric substance from every quarter of the heavens to form his own etheric body. Man was thus able to read the secrets enshrined in this etheric body from everything that was now coming to pass again between the Earth and the Cosmos. The signs of the Cosmic Word are inscribed upon the very surface of the Earth when the plants blossom and particular forms of life become manifest in the animal world at the time of Midsummer.

When Autumn approached, men saw how the letters of the Cosmic Word were again changing. At this time the warmth and light of the Sun are withdrawing and the plants are obliged to have recourse to what the Sun itself has conveyed to the Earth during Summer; in return, the Earth breathes out the blossoming life she has received during Summer but at the same time develops within herself the ripening fruit which brings the cycle of plant-life to completion, inasmuch as the plant bears within it the seed, the forces of germination. Again man was able to unveil what the Cosmic Word inscribes on the surface of the Earth herself in the ripening plants; again he was able to unriddle what the forms taken by animal life in the Autumn can reveal. He read very deep secrets of the universe in the flight of birds, in all the changes that take place in the lower animals and in the insect world as Autumn approaches. The way in which the insect world becomes silent and seeks refuge in the Earth, the changes of form it undergoes—all this conveyed to him that in Autumn the Earth is in process of withdrawing into herself, communing with herself.

This was brought to expression in certain festivals that were celebrated in the latter half of September and have still left traces in country districts in the form of the Michaelmas festival. Through these festivals man reminded himself that when all the paths in the Earth which led out into the Cosmos have failed, he must unite himself with something that is not bound up with the happenings of the physical and etheric worlds, he must turn his soul to the *spiritual* content of the Cosmos. And even in the kind of festival that is now celebrated at Michaelmas, there is still a reminiscence of humanity turning to that Spirit of the Hierarchies who will lead men in a spiritual way when external guidance through the Stars and through the Sun has lost its power.

Through everything that man read in this way in the Autumn—a reading that was also contemplation—he steeped himself in the secrets of the human astral body. Autumn was the season when those who were initiated and inspired by the Year-God read with him the secrets of the human astral body and contemplated them under his inspiration. It was at this Autumn season that the Initiates said to their pupils: "Hold fast to the Being who stands before the Face of the Sun! (The name Micha-el is still reminiscent of this.) Think of this Being, for you will need the power when you have passed through the gate of death into the supersensible worlds, when you have to go through again whatever has remained in your astral being from Earth-existence." Secrets of the human astral body were thus drawn from what revealed itself not only in the ripening, but also in the withering plants, and in the insects creeping away into the Earth. Man already knew that if they wished to make the astral body worthy of true manhood, their gaze must be turned to the spiritual worlds. It was for this reason that the souls of those who were candidates for Initiation were directed to the Being whom we can commemorate under the name of Micha-el.

But then came the season at the middle of which is our present Christmas. This was the time when those who were inspired and initiated by the Year-God pointed out to their pupils the mysteries that are revealed when water covers the Earth in the beautiful forms of snowflakes. The reading which in Autumn had already become reflection and contemplation, now became inner, active life; what in earlier seasons of the year had been observation, running parallel with the outer physical world, now became inner spiritual effort and activity. Life was deepened *inwardly*. Man knew that he can only comprehend the deepest essence of his Ego when he listens to the secrets projected by the Cosmic Word, the Cosmic Logos, into everything that takes place in Nature at the time when the Earth is swathed in her mantle of snow and when life around and on the Earth is contracted by cold. It was incumbent upon those who were initiated and

133

inspired by the Year-God to learn to understand his writing from the indications that were given in the season of Winter. Their observation was sharpened so that it could follow the processes at work in the seeds which had been laid into the Earth, and how the insects hibernate within the closely contracting forces of the Earth. Man's gaze was led from physical light into physical darkness.

There were certain Mysteries where the pupils were told: "Now you must gaze at the Midnight Sun! You must behold the Sun *through* the Earth. If the eyes of your soul are filled with the power which can follow the plants and the lower animals into the Earth, then the Earth herself will become transparent to your inmost soul." It is at the time when the Earth's forces are most contracted that man can eventually *see through* the Earth and behold the Sun as the Midnight Sun, for the Earth is now inwardly spiritualized; whereas at Midsummer, he beholds the Sun with his physical senses when he turns his gaze from the Earth to the Cosmos. To behold the Sun at the Midnight Hour in a deep Winter night was something which the pupils of the Initiates of the Year-God must learn. And it was their duty to communicate the secrets revealed to them by the Midnight Sun to those who were faithful followers of the Mysteries but could not themselves become Initiates or actual pupils of the Mysteries.

And more and more it came about in those ancient times that when the Initiates pointed to the Sun at the Midnight Hour in the depth of Winter, they were obliged to make known to their pupils that man on Earth feels his Ego deserted and forsaken in a certain way. The festival of Midwinter became for those possessed of the greatest knowledge more and more a festival of sadness and mourning through which it was to be brought home to man that within earthly existence he cannot find the way to his Ego, that he must learn from what is to be read in the signs written by the Logos on the Earth in Midwinter, how he with his Ego had been forsaken by the Cosmos. For it was the *Earth* alone of which he was aware at this time, and that for which the Ego yearns—the power of the Sun—was covered by the Earth. The Sun did indeed appear at the Midnight Hour, but man felt that the strength which would enable him to reach the Sun-Being was continually waning. At the same time, the very fact that man was made aware in this way of the loneliness of the human Ego in the Cosmos, was the prophetic indication that the Sun Being would come to the Earth, would in the course of evolution permeate the being of man, would appear in order to heal a humanity ailing on account of its loneliness in the Cosmos.

Thus even in those ancient times, intimation was given of what was to come in the evolution of man, whereby the Winter festival of sorrow and mourning would be changed —especially among the people of the South—to a festival of inner joy through the appearance of Christ upon Earth. And when this revelation descended from the Cosmos into earthly existence, those who announced the Event declared how to all men on Earth the message had gone forth that the ancient festival of mourning was now transformed into a festival of rejoicing. In the inmost depths of the Shepherds' hearts, where their dreams were woven, the words resounded: "The Godhead is revealing Himself in the Heights of the Cosmos, and peace will spring forth on Earth in men who are of good will." Such was the proclamation in the hearts of simple Shepherds.

And at the other pole, to those who were the most deeply imbued with magical knowledge, there could come from the surviving relics of ancient Star Wisdom, the message of the entry of the Cosmic Spirit into earthly matter.

Today, when we speak of the Christmas Mystery, we must think of all that is experienced through it against the background of the ancient festival of mourning; we must think of how there has entered into the course of human evolution the power by which man can wrest himself free from everything that fetters him to the Earth. We must be able to formulate the Christmas thought in such a way that we say to ourselves: The inspirations of the Year-God which revealed to the old Initiates how in the depths of Winter the Earth withdraws from the Universe and enters into a time of self-contemplation—those inspirations are still true; man can still understand how the secret of the human Ego is connected with this secret of the year. But out of his human insight, out of his discerning feeling, out of the wisdom of his heart, he can surround himself with pictures of Christ Jesus entering into the life of men on Earth, can learn to experience in all its depths the thought of the Holy Night.

But he will only be able to experience it truly if he also has the will to follow the Christ as He reveals Himself through all the ages. The task of the Initiates of the ancient Initiation-Science was to unveil the mysteries of human nature through a profound understanding of the course of the year. We too must understand what the year reveals but we must also be able to penetrate into the *inner nature of Man*. And when we do this, anthroposophical Spiritual Science shows us how the letters which are written in heart and lungs, in the brain and in every part of the human organism, unveil the secrets of the Cosmos, just as those secrets were unveiled to men inspired by the Year-God in the letters of the Logos which they read in the budding plants, in the animals, and their manner of life on the Earth. We in our time must learn to look into the inner being of Man—which must become for us a script from which we read the course of human evolution, and then devote ourselves to understanding the meaning and purpose of that evolution. Through deepened vision we must unite ourselves with the spiritual forces that weave through the evolution of humanity. And because this evolution is forever advancing, we must experience the Mystery of Golgotha, the Mystery of the Holy Night, *anew* in every epoch. We must realize the full depth of meaning contained in words spoken by the Spirit who sought out for Himself the body that was born in Bethlehem on Christmas night: "Lo, I am with you always, even to the end of the days of Earth." We must also have a spiritual ear for the perpetual revelation of the Logos through the being of Man himself. Humanity must learn to listen to the inspirations of this God of mankind, who is Christ Himself, as men learned long ago to listen to the inspirations of the Year-God.

Humanity will then not confine itself to contemplation of what is transmitted in the Bible concerning the spiritual sojourn on Earth of Christ Jesus, but will understand that ever since then, Christ has united Himself with man in earthly life, and that He reveals Himself perpetually to those who are willing to listen. Humanity in our time will then learn to understand that just as the Christmas festival once followed the Michael festival of Autumn, so the Michael-revelation which began at a time in the Autumn in the last third of the 19th century, should be followed by a sacred Christmas festival through which men will come to understand the spirit-birth needed along their path on Earth, in order that the spiritualized Earth may eventually be able to pass into future forms and conditions of existence. We are now living in an age when there should not merely be a yearly Michaelmas festival followed by a yearly Christmas festival, but when we should understand in the depths of our souls, out of our own human nature, the Michael-revelation of the last third of the 19th century, and then seek for the path leading to the *true* Christmas festival—when with increasing knowledge of the Spirit we shall be permeated by that same spirit.

Then we shall understand the words in the Gospel: "I have yet many things to say unto you, but ye cannot bear them now." Humanity is so constituted that it is capable of bearing more and more of Christ's teaching. Humanity is not intended only to listen to those who want to hinder progress, who point to what was once written down in barren letters concerning the Mystery of Golgotha, and who do not want the power of that Mystery to reveal itself to men as a living reality through the ages. Today is not the time to listen to those who would like to remain at a standstill in the Springtime of the world, which reveals outer physical nature in its brightest glory, but cannot reveal the Spiritual. Today is the time when the path must be found from the Michael festival to the Midwinter festival, when there should come to pass a *Sunrise of the Spirit.* We shall never find this path if in the evolution of man on the Earth we surrender to the illusion that there is light in external life, in external civilization, in external culture today; we must realize that in those spheres there is darkness. But in this darkness we must seek for the light which it was Christ's will to bring into the world through Jesus.

Let us then follow, with the same devotion with which the Shepherds and the Magi from the East sought the way to the Manger on that Christmas night—with the same devotion let us follow the signs which can be read in the being of man himself, in letters that are still indistinct, but will become clearer and clearer. Then it will be granted to us to celebrate anew the Christ Mystery of the Holy Night

. . . but only if we have the will to seek *in the darkness* for the light.

Today we often call by the name of 'science,' not that which explains the world but which instead of bringing light, sheds darkness and obscurity. These darknesses must reach out and take hold of the light!

If men do but try with depth and tenderness of feeling and with strongest power of will to find in the darkness the light of the Spirit, then that light will shine as did the Stars of heaven when the birth of Jesus was announced to the Shepherds and the Magi.

We must learn to place the Christmas thought into the historic evolution of humanity. We have not to wait for a new Messiah, for a new Christ. Much has been revealed to humanity through Nature—which in the course of the last few centuries has been leading men deep into the darkness of matter—and we must wait for what can now be revealed to humanity through understanding of the ever-living Christ Jesus.

We must not fasten the Christmas thought in a conventional yearly festival, but make it fluid and radiant, so that it will shine for us as did the Star at Bethlehem.

It was of this Light, this radiant Star, that I wished to speak to you, my dear friends, on this Christmas Eve. I would like to have done something to ensure that with the will that is inspired in you by anthroposophical Spiritual Science, you will unite that other will to follow the Star which in very truth shines forth to man all through the Holy Night. In deep and intimate stillness to permeate oneself with this Light—that is the deepest and truest Christmas consecration for our time. Everything else is in reality no more than an outward sign for this true Christmas feeling which we can carry over from this Christmas evening to

139

Christmas morning tomorrow. Then this Holy Night can be for us not merely a symbol but a symbol that can become a living force. And we shall also be mindful of how deeply we ought to unite with the spiritual striving that in all good men leads on into the future, and at the same time is the true Christmas striving—the striving towards that Spirit who willed to incarnate in the body born in Bethlehem on the historic Christmas Night.

III

From Man's Living Together with the Course of Cosmic Existence Arises the Cosmic Cult.

Dornach, December 29, 1922

THE object of the lectures I gave here immediately before Christmas was to indicate man's connection with the whole Cosmos and especially with the forces of spirit-and-soul pervading the Cosmos. Today I shall again be dealing with the subject-matter of those lectures but in a way that will constitute an entirely independent study.

The life of man, as far as it consists of experiences of outer Nature as well as of the inner life of soul and spirit, lies between two poles; and many of the thoughts which necessarily come to man about his connection with the world are influenced by the realization that these two polar opposites exist.

On the one side, man's life of thinking and feeling is confronted by what is called 'natural necessity.' He feels himself dependent upon adamantine laws which he finds everywhere in the world outside him and which also penetrate through him, inasmuch as his physical and also his etheric organisms are part and parcel of this outer world. On the other hand, he is deeply sensible—it is a feeling that is bound to arise in every healthy-minded person—that his dignity as man would not be fully attained if freedom were not an integral element in his life between birth and death. *Necessity* and *freedom* are the polar opposites in his life.

You are aware that in the age of natural science—the sub-

ject with which I am dealing in another course of lectures*
here there is a strong tendency to extend the sway of necessity that is everywhere in evidence in external Nature, to
whatever originates in the human being himself, and many
representative scientists have come to regard freedom as an
impossibility, an illusion that exists only in the human soul,
because when a man is faced with having to make a decision,
reasons for and reasons against it work upon him. These
reasons themselves are, however, under the sway of necessity;
hence—so say these scientists—it is really not the man who
makes the decision but whatever reasons are the more numerous and the weightier. They triumph over the other less
numerous and less weighty reasons, which also affect him.
Man is therefore carried along helplessly by the victors in
the struggle between impulses that work upon him of necessity. Many representatives of this way of thinking have
said that a man believes himself to be free only because the
polarically opposite reasons for and against any decision he
may be called upon to make, present such complications in
their totality that he does not notice how he is being tossed
hither and thither; one category of reasons finally triumphs;
one scale in a delicately poised balance is weighed down and
he is carried along in accordance with it.

Against this argument there is not only the ethical consideration that the dignity of man would not be maintained
in a world where he was merely a plaything of conflicting
yes-and-no impulses, but there is also this fact, that the
feeling of freedom in the human will is so strong that an
unbiased person has no sort of doubt that if he can be misled
as to its existence, he can equally well be misled by the most

* *The Birth of Natural Science in World-History and Its Subsequent
Development*. Course of 9 lectures given at Dornach from 24th December,
1922 to 6th January, 1923.

elementary sense-perceptions. If the elementary experience of freedom in the sphere of feeling could prove to be deceptive, so too could the experience of red, for instance, or of C or C sharp and so on. Many representatives of modern natural scientific thought place such a high value upon *theory* that they allow the theory of a natural necessity which is absolute, has no exceptions and embraces human actions and human will, to tempt them into disregarding altogether an experience such as the sense of freedom!

But this problem of necessity and freedom, with all the phenomena associated with it in the life of soul—and these phenomena are very varied and numerous—is a problem linked with much more profound aspects of universal existence than are accessible to natural science or to the everyday experience of the human soul. For at a time when man's outlook was quite different from what it is today, this disquieting, perplexing problem was already a concern of his soul.

You will have gathered from the other course of lectures now being given here that the natural scientific thinking of the modern age is by no means so very old. When we go back to earlier times we find views of the world that were as one-sidedly *spiritual* as they have become one-sidely naturalistic today. The farther back we go, the less of what is called 'necessity' do we find in man's thinking. Even in early Greek thought there was nothing of what we today call necessity, for the Greek idea of necessity had an essentially different meaning. But if we go still farther back we find, instead of necessity, the working of forces, and these, in their whole compass, were ascribed to a divine-spiritual *Providence*. Expressing myself rather colloquially, I would say that to a modern scientific thinker, the Nature-forces do everything; whereas the thinker of olden times conceived of everything being done by spiritual forces working with purposes and aims as man himself does, only with purposes far more comprehensive than those of man could ever be. Yet even with this view of the world, entirely spiritual as it was, man turned his attention to the way in which his will was subject to divine-spiritual forces; and just as today, when his thinking is in line with natural science he feels himself subject to the forces and laws of Nature, so in those ancient times he felt himself subject to divine-spiritual forces and laws. And for many who in those days were determinists in this sense, human freedom, although it is a direct experience of the soul, was no more valid than it is for our modern naturalists. These modern naturalists believe that necessity works through the actions of men; the men of olden times thought that divine-spiritual forces, in accordance with their purposes, work through human actions.

It is only necessary to recognize that the problem of freedom and necessity exists in these two completely opposite worlds of thought to realize that quite certainly no examination of the surface-aspect of conditions and happenings can lead to any solution of this problem which penetrates so deeply into all life and into all evolution.

We must look more deeply into the process of world-evolution—world-evolution as the course of Nature on the one side and as the unfolding of spirit on the other—before it is possible to grasp the whole meaning and implications of a problem as vital as this; insight can indeed only come from anthroposophical thinking.

The course of Nature is usually studied in an extremely restricted way. Isolated happenings and processes of a highly specialized kind are studied in the laboratories, brought within the range of telescopes or subjected to experiment.

This means that observation of the course of Nature and of world-evolution is confined within very narrow limits. And those who study the domain of soul and spirit imitate the scientists and naturalists. They fight shy of taking into account the *whole* man when they are considering his life of soul. Instead of this they specialize in order to accentuate some particular thought or sentient experience with important bearings, and hope in this way eventually to build up a psychology, just as efforts are made to build up a body of knowledge of the physical world out of single observations and experiments conducted in chemical and physical laboratories, in clinics and so forth.

Yet in reality these studies never lead to any comprehensive understanding either of the physical world or of the world of soul-and-spirit. As little as it is the intention here to disparage the justification of these specialized investigations—for they *are* justified from points of view often referred to in my lectures—as strongly it must be emphasized that unless the world itself, unless Nature herself reveals to man somewhere or other what results from the interworking of the details, he will never be able to build up from his single observations and experiments a picture of the structure of the world that is confirmed by the actual happenings. Liver cells and minute activities of the liver, brain-cells and minute cerebral processes can be investigated and greater and greater specialization may take place in these domains; but these investigations, because they lead to particularization and not to the whole, will give no help towards forming a view of the human organism in its totality, unless from the very beginning a man has a comprehensive, intuitive idea of this totality to help him in forming the separate investigations into a unified whole. In like manner, as long as chemistry, astro-chemistry, physics, astro-physics, biology, restrict themselves to the investigation of isolated details, they will never be able to give a picture of how the different forces and laws in our world-environment work together to form a whole, unless man develops the faculty of perceiving in Nature outside something similar to what can be seen as the totality of the human organism, in which all the separate processes of liver, kidneys, hearts, brain, and so forth, are included. In other words, we must be able to point to something in the universe in which all the forces we behold in our environment *work together to form a self-contained whole.*

Now it may be that certain processes in the human liver and human brain will not for a long time to come be detected with enough accuracy to be accepted by biology. But at all events, as long as men have been able to look at other men, they have always said: The processes of liver, stomach, heart, etc. work together within the boundary of the skin to form a whole. Without being obliged to look at each and all of the separate details, we have before us the sum-total of the chemical, physical and biological processes belonging to man's nature.

Is it possible also to have before us as a complete whole the sum-total of the forces and laws of Nature that are at work around us? In a certain way it *is* possible. But in order not to be misunderstood I must emphasize the fact that such totalities are always relative. For instance, we can group together the processes of the outer ear and then have a relative whole. But we can also group together the processes in that part of the organ of hearing which continues on to the brain and then we have another relative whole; taking the two groups together, we have another, greater whole, which in turn belongs to the head, and this again to the whole organism. And it will be just the same when we

146

try to comprehend in one complete picture the laws and forces that come primarily into consideration for man.

A first complete whole of this kind is the cycle of *day and night*. Paradoxical as this seems at first hearing, in this cycle of day and night a number of natural laws around us are gathered together into one whole. During the course of a day and night, processes are going on in our environment and penetrating through us which, if separated out, prove to be physical and chemical processes of every possible different kind. We can say: The cycle of the day is a *time-organism*, a time-organism embracing a number of natural processes which can be studied individually.

A greater 'totality' is the course of the year. If we review all the changes which affect the earth and mankind during the course of the year in the sphere surrounding us—in the atmosphere, for example—we shall find that all the processes taking place in the plants and also in the minerals from one Spring to the next, form in their *time-sequence* an organic whole, although otherwise they reveal themselves to us and also to different scientific investigations as separate phenomena. They form a whole, just as the processes taking place in the liver, kidneys, spleen and so forth form a whole in the human organism. The course of the year is actually an organic whole—the expression is not quite exact but words of some kind have to be used—the year is an organic sum-total of occurrences and facts which it is customary in natural science to investigate singly.

Speaking in what sounds a rather trivial way, but you will realize that the meaning is very profound, we might say: if man is to avoid having to surrounding Nature the very abstract relationship he adopts to descriptions of chemical and physical experiments, or to what is often taught today in botany and zoology, the time-organisms of the course of the day and the course of the year must become realities for him—realities of cosmic existence. He will then find in them a certain kinship with his own constitution.

Let us begin by thinking of the *cycle of the year*. Reviewing it as we did in the lecture before Christmas, we find a whole series of processes in the sprouting, growing plants which first produce leaves and, later on, blossoms. An incalculable number of natural processes reveal themselves from the life in the root, on into the life in the green leaves and in the colored petals. And we have an altogether different kind of process before us when we see, in Autumn, the fading, withering and dying of outer Nature.

The cosmic happenings around us form an organic unity. In Summer we see how the Earth opens out all her organs to the Cosmos and how her life and activities rise towards the cosmic expanse. This applies not only to the plant world but to the animal world too in a certain sense— especially to the lower animals. Think of all the activity in the insect world during the Summer, how this activity seems to rise up from the Earth and is given over to the Cosmos, especially to the forces coming from the Sun. During Autumn and Winter we see how everything that from the time of Spring onwards reached out towards the cosmic expanse, falls back again into the earthly realm, how the Earth as it were gradually increases her hold upon all growing life, brings it to the stage of apparent death, or at least to a state of sleep—how the Earth closes all her organs against the influences of the Cosmos. Here we have two contrasting processes in the course of the year, embracing countless details but nevertheless representing a complete whole.

If with the eyes of the soul we contemplate this yearly cycle, which can be regarded as a complete whole because

148

from a certain point it simply repeats itself, recurring in approximately the same way, we find in it nothing else than Nature-necessity. And in our own earthly lives we human beings follow this Nature-necessity. If our lives followed it *entirely* we should be completely under its domination. Now it is certainly true that those forces of Nature which come especially into consideration for us as Earth-dwellers are present in the course of the year; for the Earth does not change so quickly that the minute changes taking place from year to year make themselves noticeable during a man's life, however old he may live to be.—So by living each year through Spring, Summer, Autumn and Winter, we partake with our own bodies in Nature-necessity.

It is important to think in this way, for it is only actual experience that gives knowledge; no theory ever does so. Every theory starts from some special domain and then proceeds to generalize. True knowledge can only be acquired when we start from life and from experience. We must not therefore consider the laws of gravity *by themselves,* or the laws of plant life, or the laws of animal instinct, or the laws of mental coercion, because if we do, we think only of their details, generalize them, and then arrive at entirely false conclusions. We must have in mind where the Nature-forces are revealed in their cooperation and mutual interaction— and that is in the *cyclic course of the year.*

Now even supervisial study shows that man is relatively free in his relation to the course of the year, but Anthroposophy shows this even more clearly. In Anthroposophy we turn our attention to the two alternating conditions in which every human being lives during the 24 hours of the day, namely, the sleeping state and the waking state. We know that during the waking state the physical, etheric and astral bodies and the Ego-organism form a relative unity in the

149

human being. In the sleeping state the physical and etheric bodies remain behind in the bed, closely interwoven, and the Ego and the astral body are outside the physical and etheric bodies.

If with the means provided by anthroposophical research —of which you will have read in our literature—we study the physical and etheric bodies of man during sleep and during waking life, the following comes to light. When the Ego and the astral body are outside the physical and etheric organism during sleep, a kind of life begins in the latter which is to be found in external Nature in the mineral and plant kingdoms only. And the reason why the physical and etheric organisms of man do not gradually pass over into a sum-total of plant or mineral processes is simply due to the fact that the Ego and astral body are within them for certain periods. If the return of the Ego and astral body were too long delayed, the physical and etheric bodies would pass over into a mineral and vegetative form of life. As it is, a *tendency* to become vegetative and mineralized commences in man after he falls asleep, and this tendency has the upper hand during sleeping life.

If with the insight afforded by anthroposophical research, we contemplate the human being while he is asleep, we see in him—of course with the inevitable variations—a faithful copy of what the Earth is throughout Spring and Summer. Mineral and vegetative life begins to bud in him, although naturally in quite a different way from what happens in the green plants which grow out of the Earth. Nevertheless, with one variation, what goes on during sleep in the physical and etheric organism of man is a faithful image of the period of Spring and Summer on the Earth. In this respect, the organism of man of the present epoch is in tune with external Nature. His physical eyes can survey it. He beholds its

150

sprouting, budding life. As soon as he attains to *Inspiration* and *Imagination,* a picture of Summer is revealed to him when physical man is asleep. In sleep, Spring and Summer are there for the physical and etheric bodies of man. A budding, sprouting life begins. And when we wake, when the Ego and astral body returns, all this budding life in the physical and etheric bodies withdraws and for the eye of seership, life in the physical and etheric organism begins to be very similar to the life of the Earth during Autumn and Winter. When we follow the human being through one complete period of sleeping and waking life, we have before us in miniature an actual microcosmic reflection of Spring, Summer, Autumn and Winter. If we follow man's physical and etheric organism through a period of 24 hours, contemplating it in the light of Spiritual Science, we pass, in the microcosmic sense, through the course of a year. Accordingly, if we consider only that part of man which remains behind in the bed when he is asleep or moves around when he is awake during the day, we can say that the course of the year is completed microcosmically in him.

But now let us consider the other part of man's being which releases itself in sleep—the Ego and astral body. If again we use the kinds of knowledge available in spiritual investigation, namely Inspiration and Intuition, we shall find that the Ego and astral body are given over while man is asleep to spiritual Powers within which they will not, in the normal condition, be able to live *consciously* until a later epoch of the Earth's existence. From the time of going to sleep until the time of waking, the Ego and astral body are withdrawn from the world just as the Earth is withdrawn from the Cosmos during Winter. During sleep, Ego and astral body are actually in their Winter period. So that in the being of man during sleep there is an intermingling of

151

conditions which are only present at one and the same time on *opposite* hemispheres of the Earth's surface; for during sleep man's physical and etheric bodies have their Summer and his Ego and astral body their Winter.

During waking life, conditions are reversed. The physical and etheric organism is then in its Winter period. The Ego and astral body are given over to what can stream from the Cosmos to man in his waking state. So when the Ego and astral body come down into the physical and etheric organism, they (i.e. Ego and astral body) have their Summer period. Once more we have the two seasons side by side, but now Winter in the physical and etheric organism, Summer in the Ego and astral body.

On the Earth, Summer and Winter cannot be intermingled. But in man, the microcosm, Summer and Winter intermingle all the time. When man is asleep his physical Summer mingles with spiritual Winter; when he is awake his physical Winter mingles with spiritual Summer. In external Nature, Summer and Winter are separated in the course of the year. In man, Summer and Winter mingle all the time from two different directions. In external Nature on Earth, Winter and Summer follow one another in time. In the human being, Winter and Summer are simultaneous, only they interchange, so that at one time there is Spirit-Summer together with Body-Winter (waking life), and at another, Spirit-Winter together with Body-Summer (sleeping life).

Thus the laws and forces in external Nature around us cannot neutralize each other in any one region of the Earth, because they work in sequence, the one after the other in time; but in man they *do* neutralize each other. The course of Nature is such that just as through two opposing forces a state of rest can be brought about, so can an untold number of natural laws neutralize and cancel out each other. This

152

happens in the human being with respect to all laws of external Nature, inasmuch as he sleeps and wakes in the regular way. The two conditions which appear as Nature-necessity only when they succeed each other in time, are coincident and consequently neutralized in man—and *it is this that makes him a free being.*

Freedom can never be understood until it is realized how the Summer and Winter forces of man's spiritual life can neutralize the Summer and Winter forces of his outer physical and etheric nature.

External Nature presents to us pictures which we must *not* see in ourselves, either in the waking or in the sleeping state. On no account must this happen. On the contrary, we must say that these pictures of the course and order of Nature *lose their validity* within the constitution of man, and we must turn our gaze elsewhere. For when the course of Nature within the human being no longer disturbs us, it becomes possible for the first time to gaze at man's spiritual, moral and psychic make-up. And then we begin to have an ethical and moral relationship to him, just as we have a corresponding relationship to Nature.

When we contemplate our own being with the aid of knowledge acquired in this way, we find, telescoped into one another, conditions which in the external world are spread across the stream of time. And there are many other things of which the same could be said. If we contemplate our inner being and understand it rightly in the sense I have indicated today, we bring it into a relationship with the course of time different from the one to which we are accustomed today.

The purely external mode of scientific observation does not reach the stage where the investigator can say: In the being of man you must hear sounding together what can only be heard as separate tones in the flow of Time.—But if you develop spiritual hearing, the tones of Summer and Winter can be heard ringing simultaneously in man, and they are the same tones that we hear in the outer world when we enter into the flow of Time itself. *Time becomes Space.* The whole surrounding universe also resounds to us in Time: expanded widely in Space, there ring forth what resounds from our own being as from a centre, gathered as it were, in a single point.

This is the moment, my dear friends, when scientific study and contemplation becomes artistic study and contemplation: when art and science no longer stand in stark contrast as they do in our naturalistic age, but when they are interrelated in the way sensed by Goethe when he said that art reveals those secrets of Nature without which we can never fully understand her. From a certain point onwards it is imperative that we should understand the form and structure of the world as *artistic creation.* And once we have taken the path from the purely scientific conception of the world to artistic understanding, we shall also be ready to take the third step, which leads to a deepening of religious experience.

When we have found the physical forces and the forces of soul-and-spirit working together in the inner centre of our being, we can also behold them in the Cosmos. Human willing rises to the level of artistic creative power and finally achieves a relationship to the world that is not merely passive knowledge but *positive, active surrender.* Man no longer looks at the world abstractly, with the forces of his head, but his vision becomes more and more an activity of his *whole* being. Living together with the course of cosmic existence becomes a happening different in character from his connection with the facts and events of everyday life. It becomes a ritual, a cult, and the cosmic ritual comes into being in which man can have his place at every moment of his life. Every earthly cult and ritual is a symbolic image of this cosmic cult and ritual—which is higher and more sublime than all earthly cults.

If what has been said today has been thoroughly grasped, it will be possible to study the relationship of the anthroposophical outlook to any particular religious cult. And this will be done during the next few days, when we shall consider the relationship between Anthroposophy and different forms of cult.

IV

*The Relation of the Movement for Religious Renewal
to the Anthroposophical Movement.*

I HAVE often said in this place that in more ancient
times in the evolution of humanity, science, art, and religion
formed a harmonious unity. Anyone who is able in one way
or another to gain knowledge of the nature of the ancient
Mysteries knows that within these Mysteries, knowledge was
sought as a revelation of the Spiritual in picture form, in the
way that was possible in those times. That way can no longer
be ours, although in this age we must again advance to a
knowledge of the spiritual nature of the world. A pictorial
knowledge of the Spiritual lay at the foundation of all ancient
conceptions of the world. This knowledge came to direct
expression, not merely by being communicated in words, but
through forms which have gradually become those of our
arts—bodily, plastic presentation in the plastic arts and presentation by means of tone and word in the arts of music and
speech. But this second stage was followed by the third
stage, that of the revelation of the nature of the world in
religious cult or ritual, a revelation through which the *whole*
man felt himself uplifted to the divine-spiritual ground of
the world, not merely in thought, nor merely in feeling as
happens through art, but in such a way that thoughts, feelings
and also the inmost impulses of the will surrendered themselves in reverent devotion to this divine-spiritual principle.

Dornach, December 30, 1922

156

And the sacred acts and rites were the means whereby the external actions of man's will were to be filled with spirit. Men felt the living unity in science (as it was then conceived), art, and religion. The ideal of the spiritual life of the present day must be, once more to gain knowledge that can bring to realization what Goethe already divined: a *knowledge* that raises itself to *art,* not symbolical or allegorical art, but true art—which means creative, formative activity in tones and in words—an art which also deepens into direct *religious experience.*

Only when anthroposophical Spiritual Science is seen to contain this impulse within it, is its true being understood. Obviously humanity will have to take many steps in spiritual development before such an ideal can be realized. But it is just the patient devotion to the taking of these steps which must bring blessing to the Anthroposophical Movement.

Now I should like, in the series of lectures now being given, to speak from one particular aspect on this impulse in the Anthroposophical Movement to which reference has just been made. Perhaps, my dear friends, at the close of what I have to say, you will understand what is really the deeper cause of my words. Let me say in the first place that already for a long time now the Anthroposophical Movement has not coincided with the Anthroposophical Society, but that the Anthroposophical Society, if it would fulfill its task, must really carry the whole impulse of the Anthroposophical Movement. The Anthroposophical Movement has laid hold of wider circles than merely the Anthroposophical Society. Hence it has come about that in more recent years the way of working had necessarily to be different for the Anthroposophical Movement from what it was when the Anthroposophical Movement was essentially contained within the

157

Anthroposophical Society. But the Anthroposophical Society can only fulfill its real nature when it feels itself as the kernel of the Anthroposophical Movement.

Now in order not to speak merely theoretically but to make what I have just said really intelligible, I must tell you a little about something that has recently taken place in connection with a Movement that is distinct from the Anthroposophical Movement, because, if I did not do this, misunderstanding might easily arise.

I will therefore narrate briefly the manner in which a certain Movement having a religious, cultic character has arisen, a Movement which indeed has much to do with the Anthroposophical Movement, but should not be confused with it: it is the religious movement which calls itself 'The Movement for Religious Renewal,' * for the renewal of Christianity. The position of this Movement with respect to the Anthroposophical Movement will become clear if we take our start from the forms in which this Movement for Religious Renewal has developed.

Some time ago a few enthusiastic young theological students came to me. They were about to conclude their theological studies and enter upon the practical duties of ministers of religion. What they said to me was to the following effect: When at the present time a student receives with a really devoted Christian heart the theology offered to him at the universities, he feels at last as if he had no firm ground under his feet for the practical work of a minister that is before him. The theology and religion of our time has gradually assumed forms that do not really enable it to instil into its ministers for their practical work and their care of souls the impulse that must proceed as a living power from the Mystery

* This Movement was the beginning of *The Christian Community* as it has since been called.

of Golgotha, from the consciousness that the Christ Being Who formerly lived in spiritual worlds, has since united Himself with human life on earth and now works on further in that life.—I perceived that in the souls of those who came to me there was the feeling that if Christianity is to be kept alive, a renewal of the entire theological impulse and of the entire religious impulse is necessary; otherwise Christianity cannot be the really vital force for our whole spiritual life. And it is indeed clear that the religious impulse only assumes its true significance and meaning when it lays hold of a man so deeply that it pervades everything he brings forth out of his thinking, feeling, and will.

I remarked first of all to those who came to me in this way for help in what they were seeking and could only find where anthroposophical Spiritual Science is making its way into the world today—I pointed out to them that one cannot work from the enthusiasm of a few single individuals, but that it is a question of gathering together, as it were, similar strivings in wider circles, even though the striving may be more or less unconscious. I said to these people that theirs was obviously not an isolated striving; rather was it the case that they were feeling in their hearts—perhaps more intensely than others—what countless human beings of the present day are also feeling; and I showed them that if it is a question of religious renewal, one must start from a broad basis whereon can be found a large number of persons out of whose hearts springs the impulse to strive for that renewal.

After a while the people in question came to me again. They had fully accepted what I had said to them and now they were able to tell me that they had been joined by a considerable number of other young theological students who were in the same position, that is to say, who were dissatisfied with the present theological and religious aims at the universities and yet were about to enter upon the practical duties of ministers of the church; and there seemed every prospect of the circle being increased.

I said: It is quite obvious first of all that it is not only a question of having a band of preachers and ministers, but into such a movement for religious renewal should be drawn not only those who can teach and perform the duties of pastors, but above all those—and they are very numerous—who possess more or less dimly in their hearts a strong religious impulse, a specifically Christian impulse, which, in view of the way in which theological religion has developed, cannot be satisfied. I pointed out, therefore, that there are circles of people in the population who are not within the Anthroposophical Movement, and who, from the whole tenor of their mind and heart, do not immediately find their way to the Anthroposophical Movement.

I remarked further, that for the Anthroposophical Movement it is ultimately a case of seeing clearly and distinctly that we are living in an age when, simply through the world's evolution, a number of spiritual truths, truths regarding the actual spiritual content of the world, can be found by men when they become spiritual researchers. And if men do not become spiritual researchers but strive after the truth in the way in which it must disclose itself to man when he is conscious of his human dignity, then the truths discovered by spiritual researchers can be understood by such persons by means of their ordinary, sound human intellect—provided it is *really* sound.

I went on to say that the Anthroposophical Movement is founded upon the principle that he who finds his way into it knows that what is important above all is that the spiritual truths now accessible to humanity should lay hold of men's hearts and minds as *knowledge*. The essential thing is that *knowledge* should enter the spiritual life of man. It is of course not the case that one who is in the Anthroposophical Movement need be versed in the various sciences. One may be in the Anthroposophical Movement without possessing any impulse or any inclination towards natural science, for the truths of Anthroposophy are perfectly comprehensible to the human intellect if only it is healthy and unclouded by prejudice. If already at the present time a sufficiently large number of persons out of the natural tendencies of their heart and mind were to find their way to the Anthroposophical Movement, then *all that is necessary for religious aims and religious ideals would also gradually develop together with anthroposophical knowledge out of the Anthroposophical Movement.* But there are, as I have already said, a great number of people who have the above-mentioned urge towards a renewal of religion, that is to say towards a renewal of Christian religion, and who, simply through being in certain circles of the cultural life, cannot find their way into the Anthroposophical Movement. What is necessary for these people at the present time is that a path suited to them should be found, leading to the spiritual life appropriate to the humanity of the present day.

I pointed out that it was a matter of forming communities; that what is to be reached in Anthroposophy can be attained first of all in the single individual, but that, out of the knowledge thus gained in an individual way, there must flow by an absolute inner necessity the ethical and religious *social* activity that is requisite for the future of humanity.

It is therefore a question of giving something to those people who are at first unable to set out directly along the path to the Anthroposophical Movement. The spiritual path

161

for them must be sought by forming communities in which heart and soul and spirit work together—a path adapted to human evolution at its present stage.

What I then had to say out of the needs of our human evolution to those persons who came to me may be summed up approximately in the words: it is necessary for the evolution of humanity at the present time that the Anthroposophical Movement should grow more and more, in accordance with the conditions which underlie it, and which consist especially in this—that the spiritual truths which want to come to us from the spiritual world should first of all enter the hearts of men directly, so that men may be strengthened by these spiritual truths. They will then find the way, which will be on the one hand an artistic way, and on the other a religious, ethical, and social way. The Anthroposophical Movement has gone along this path since its inception, and for the Anthroposophical Movement *no other path* is necessary, if only this path be rightly understood. The need for another path arises for those who cannot directly take this one, but who through community-building and corporate endeavor within the community, must follow a different path, one which only *later* will join the anthroposophical path.

In this way the prospect was opened for two movements to travel side by side. There is the Anthroposophical Movement, which attains its true aims when it adheres with intelligence and vigor to the meaning and purpose originally contained in it and is not led astray by any special fields of work that are bound to open up as time goes on. Even the field of scientific work, for example, must not encroach upon the impulse of the general Anthroposophical Movement. We must clearly understand that it is the anthroposophical impulse which constitutes the Anthroposophical Movement, and although various fields of scientific work have recently been

162

started within the Anthroposophical Movement it is absolutely necessary that the power and energy of the general anthroposophical impulse should not be weakened. In particular, the anthroposophical impulse must not be drawn into the forms of thinking and ideation prevailing in various fields of science—which ought actually to be vitalized by it—and be colored by them to such an extent that Anthroposophy becomes, let us say, chemical as Chemistry is today, physical as Physics is today, or biological as Biology is today. That must not happen on any account; it would strike at the very heart of the Anthroposophical Movement. What is essential is that the Anthroposophical Movement shall preserve its spiritual purity, but also its spiritual energy. To this end it must embody the essential nature of the anthroposophical spirituality, must live and move in it and bring forth out of the spiritual revelations of the present day everything that seeks to penetrate also into the life of science.

Side by side with this—so I said at that time—there might be such a movement for religious renewal, which of course has no significance for those who find the way into Anthroposophy, but is intended for those who, to begin with, cannot find this way. And as there are numbers of such people, a movement such as this is not only justified, but also necessary.

Taking for granted therefore that the Anthroposophical Movement *will remain what it was and what it ought to be,* I gave something, quite independently of the Anthroposophical Movement, to a number of persons who, *from their own impulse, not mine,* wished to work for the Movement for Religious Renewal; I gave what I was in a position to give in respect of what a future theology needs; and I also gave the contents of the ceremonial and ritual required by this new community.

163

What I have been able to give to these people out of the conditions pertaining to spiritual knowledge at the present time, I have given as a man to other men. What I have given them *has nothing to do with the Anthroposophical Movement*. I have given it to them as a private individual, and in such a way that I have emphasized with the necessary firmness that the Anthroposophical Movement must not have anything to do with this Movement for Religious Renewal; above all that I am *not* the founder of this Movement, and I rely upon this being made quite clear to the world; to individuals who wished to found this Movement for Religious Renewal I have given the necessary counsels—which are consonant with the practice of an authentic and inwardly vital cult, filled with spiritual content, to be celebrated in a right way with the forces out of the spiritual world. When I gave this advice I never performed a ritualistic act myself; I only showed, step by step, to those who wished to enact the ceremonies, how they have to be performed. That was necessary. And today it is also necessary that within the Anthroposophical Society *this should be correctly understood*.

The Movement for Religious Renewal, therefore, was founded independently of me, independently of the Anthroposophical Society. I only gave advice. The one who started it, the one who performed the very first ceremony in this Movement, performed it under my guidance, but I had no part whatever in the founding of this Movement. It is a Movement which originated of itself but received counsel from me because, when advice is justifiably asked in any particular sphere of work, is is a human duty, if one can give the advice, to do so.

Thus it must be understood, in the strictest sense of the word, that alongside the Anthroposophical Movement another

164

Movement has started, founded out of itself (*not* out of the Anthroposophical Movement), for the reason that outside the Anthroposophical Society there are numbers of people who cannot find their way into the Anthroposophical Movement itself, but who will be able to come to it later on. Therefore strict distinctions must be made between the Anthroposophical Movement, the Anthroposophical Society, and the Movement for Religious Renewal. And it is important that Anthroposophy should not be looked upon as the founder of this Movement for Religious Renewal.

This has nothing to do with the fact that the advice which makes this religious Movement into a real spiritual community in a form suited to the present stage of human evolution, was given in all love and also in all devotion to the spiritual Powers who are able to place such a Movement in the world today. So that this Movement has only originated in the right way when it considers what is within the Anthroposophical Movement as something that *gives it a sure ground* and when it puts its trust in the Anthroposophical Movement, and seeks help and counsel from those who are within the Anthroposophical Movement, and so on. Taking into account the fact that the opponents of the Anthroposophical Movement today consider every method of attack justifiable, points such as these must be made quite clear, and I must here declare that everyone who is honest and sincere with respect to the Anthroposophical Movement would be obliged to deny any statement to the effect that the Movement for Religious Renewal was founded at Dornach in the Goetheanum and by the Goetheanum. For that is not the case, the facts are as I have just presented them.

Thus in view of the way in which I myself have helped this Movement for Religious Renewal to find its feet, I have necessarily had to picture to myself that this Movement—

which puts its trust in the Anthroposophical Movement and regards the Anthroposophical Movement as its forerunner —will look for adherents outside the Anthroposophical Society, and that it would consider it a grave mistake to carry into the Anthroposophical Society the work and aims which are indeed necessary *outside* that Society. For the Anthroposophical Society is not understood by one who belongs to it unless his attitude is that he can be a counsellor and helper of this religious Movement, but cannot directly immerse himself in it. If he were to do so, he would be working for two ends: firstly, for the ruin and destruction of the Anthroposophical Society; secondly, to make fruitless the Movement for Religious Renewal. All the movements which arise among humanity in a justifiable way must indeed work together as in one organic whole, but this working together must take place *in the right way*. In the human organism it is quite impossible for the blood system to become nervous system, or for the nervous system to become blood system. The several systems have to work in the human organism distinct and separate from one another; it is precisely then that they will work together in the right way. It is therefore necessary that the Anthroposophical Society, with its content Anthroposophy, shall remain unweakened in any way by the other Movement; and that one who understands what the Anthroposophical Movement is, should—not in any presumptuous, arrogant sense, but as one who reckons with the tasks of the age—be able to see that those who have once found their way into the Anthroposophical Society *do not need a religious renewal*. For what would the Anthroposophical Society be if it first needed religious renewal!

But religious renewal *is* needed in the world, and because it is needed, because it is a profound necessity, a hand was extended to aid in founding it. Matters will therefore go on in the right way if the Anthroposophical Society remains as it is, if those who wish to understand it grasp its essential nature and do not think that it is necessary for them to belong to another movement which has taken what it possesses from Anthroposophy—although it is true in a real sense that Anthroposophy has not founded this Movement for Religious Renewal but that it has founded itself.

Anyone therefore who does not clearly distinguish these things and keep them apart, is actually—by becoming lax as regards the essential impulse of the Anthroposophical Movement—working for the destruction of the Anthroposophical Movement and for the removal of the ground and backbone of the Movement for Religious Renewal. If anyone who stands on the ground of the Movement for Religious Renewal thinks he must extend this Movement to the Anthroposophical Movement, he removes the ground from under his own feet. For everything of the nature of cult and ritual is finally bound to dissolve away when the 'backbone' of knowledge is broken.

For the welfare of both Movements it is essential that they should be held clearly apart. Therefore in the beginning, since everything depends on our developing the strength to carry out what we have set our will to do, it is absolutely necessary in these early days that the Movement for Religious Renewal should work in all directions in circles *outside* the Anthroposophical Movement; that therefore, neither as regards the acquisition of material means—in order that the matter be clearly understood I must also speak about these things—should it encroach on sources which in any event only flow with great difficulty for the Anthroposophical Movement, nor, because it does not at once succeed in finding adherents among non-Anthroposophists, should it, for example, make proselytes within the ranks of the Anthroposophists. Were it to do so, it would be doing something that would inevitably lead to the destruction of both Movements. It is really not a matter today of going forward with a certain fanaticism, but of being conscious that we can do what is necessary for man *only* when we work out of the necessity of the thing itself.

What I am now stating as consequences, were also equally the *preliminary conditions* for lending my assistance in the founding of the Movement for Religious Renewal, for only under these conditions could I assist it. If these preliminary conditions had not been there, the Movement for Religious Renewal would never have originated through my advice.

Therefore I beg you to understand that it is necessary for the Movement for Religious Renewal to know that it must adhere to its starting point, that it has promised to look for its adherents outside the sphere of the Anthroposophical Movements, for it is there that they can be found in the natural way, and there they must be sought.

What I have said to you has not been said because of any anxiety lest something might be dug away from the Anthroposophical Movement, and it has certainly not been said out of any personal motive, but solely out of the necessity of the case itself. And it is also important to understand *in what way alone* it is possible to work rightly in each of these spheres of activity. It is indeed necessary that with regard to important matters we should state quite clearly how the case stands, for there is at the present time far too great a tendency to blur things and not to see them clearly. But clarity is essential today in every sphere.

If therefore someone were to exclaim: The very one who himself put this Movement for Religious Renewal into the world now speaks like this!! . . . well, my dear friends, the whole point is that if I had at any time spoken differently about these things, I should not have lent a hand towards founding this Movement for Religious Renewal. It must remain at its starting point. What I am now saying, I am of course saying merely in order that these things may be correctly understood in the Anthroposophical Society and so that it shall not be said (as is reported to have happened already) : The Anthroposophical Movement did not get on very well, and so now they have founded the Movement for Religious Renewal as the right thing.

I am quite sure that the very excellent and outstanding individuals who have founded the Movement for Religious Renewal will oppose any such legend most vigorously, and will also sternly refuse to make proselytes within the Anthroposophical Movement.—But, as has been said, the matter must be rightly understood within the Anthroposophical Movement itself.

I know, my dear friends, that there are always some who find it unpleasant to hear explanations such as these—which are necessary from time to time, not in order to complain in one direction or another, nor for the sake of criticism, but solely in order to present something once and for all in its true light. I know there are always some who dislike it when clarity is substituted for nebulous obscurity. But this is absolutely essential for the welfare and growth of the Anthroposophical Movement as well as of the Movement for Religious Renewal. The *Movement for Religious Renewal cannot flourish if it in any way damages the Anthroposophical Movement.*

This must be thoroughly understood, especially by Anthroposophists, so that whenever it is necessary to stand up for the rights of the matter, they may really be able to do so.

169

When, therefore, there is any question about an anthroposophist's attitude towards religious renewal, he must be clear that his attitude can only be that of an adviser, that he gives what he can give in the way of spiritual possessions, and when it is a case of participating in the ceremonies, that he is conscious of doing so in order to help these ceremonies on their way. He alone can be a spiritual helper of the Movement for Religious Renewal who is himself first a good anthroposophist. But this Movement for Religious Renewal must be sustained, in every direction, by persons who, because of the particular configuration and tendencies of their spiritual life, cannot yet find their way into the Anthroposophical Society itself.

I hope that none of you will now go to someone who is doing active work in the Movement for Religious Renewal and say: This or that has been said against it in Dornach.—Nothing has been said against it. In love and in devotion to the spiritual world the Movement for Religious Renewal has been given counsel from out of the spiritual world, in order that it might rightly found itself. But the fact must be known by Anthroposophists that it has founded itself out of itself, that it has formed—not, it is true, the content of its ritual, but the *fact* of its ritual, out of its own force and its own initiative, and that the essential core of the Anthroposophical Movement has nothing to do with the Movement for Religious Renewal.

Certainly no wish could be stronger than mine that the Movement for Religious Renewal shall grow and flourish more and more, but always in adherence to the original intentions. Anthroposophical Groups must not be changed into communities for religious renewal, either in a material or in a spiritual sense.

I was obliged to say this today, for, as you know, counsel and advice had to be given for a Cult, a Cult whose growth in our present time is earnestly desired by me. In order that no misunderstanding should arise in regard to *this* Cult when I speak tomorrow of the conditions of the life of Cult in the spiritual world, I felt it necessary to insert these words today as an episode in our course of lectures.

V

*'Spiritual Knowledge is a True Communion, the
Beginning of a Cosmic Cult Suitable
for Men of the Present Age.'*

Dornach, New Year's Eve, 1922-3
(The fire which destroyed the First Goetheanum was discovered one hour after this lecture had finished.)

THE day before yesterday I spoke of how the cycle
of the year can also be found in man. I pointed out that the
forces of Nature around us group themselves into a sort of
time-organism which we call the cycle of a year, so that we
can see, during the course of a year, the interaction and cooperation of occurrences which otherwise appear like isolated
processes and facts in Nature.

Now the essential difference between this Nature-cycle
and its image in man is that events which take place *suc-
cessively* in a particular region of the Earth, take place *con-
currently* in man. Man, it is true, taken as a whole, resembles
the Earth-globe taken as a whole, inasmuch as when it is
Winter in one hemisphere it is Summer in the other, and
so forth. In the case of the Earth, however, if we take the
Winter influences as they work in one region and the simultaneous Summer influences working in another region, the
two flow away from one another and neither is disturbed or
weakened in its operation by the other. But now consider
how it is with man. When he is asleep, his physical and

172

etheric bodies are in a kind of Summer condition—a budding and sprouting life. Spiritual sight shows us this budding and sprouting Summer condition of man's physical and etheric bodies during sleep, when the Ego and astral body are separated from them. We can say that while man is asleep, there is a kind of successive Spring and Summer condition in the physical and etheric organism which he has left behind. At the same time the Ego and astral body, which still co-operate in supporting the human organism as a whole, are in a sort of Winter condition. Thus here again there are simultaneous Summer and Winter conditions, but in man they are not turned away from one another; on the contrary, they work into one another. And it is the same in our waking life. As long as man is awake, his physical and etheric bodies are in a kind of Autumn and Winter condition. Their organic life is waning, so to speak. On the other hand the Ego and the astral body, stirred by external impressions and by the thoughts to which these impressions give rise in man, are in full Summer or full Spring conditions. So that once more we find inner Spring, inner Summer and inner Winter working together in man, not turning away from one another, but irradiating each other.

This is what actually takes place, as disclosed by the researches of Spiritual Science. If we wished to compare the entire Earth with man in respect to Winter and Summer, we should have to turn the Summer in the one hemisphere right round and superimpose it on the Winter in the other hemisphere. Were this possible we should have actually what may be described as Summer conditions cancelling Winter conditions, and Winter conditions cancelling Summer conditions —producing a kind of equilibrium. Now this is an important fact, not yet realized by external science, which in consequence is bound to misunderstand the essential nature of man.

173

For in man, Summer and Winter—if I may allow myself the expression, for it really corresponds to what actually takes place—cancel one another.

It is true that man bears surrounding Nature in himself, but its activities cancel one another and a condition sets in which actually brings the activities of Nature to a state of rest. Even as in a balance that has weights in either scale, the pointer will come to rest at a certain spot and will at that spot be affected neither by the weight to the right nor by the weight to the left, but there will be equilibrium in respect to the forces which otherwise affect the beam, so there is in man a counterpoise resulting from opposing natural forces.

Anyone who studies what I said very briefly in my book *Riddles of the Soul,* about man as a threefold being—studying it really carefully, as people are not yet accustomed to do—will find that what I am now going to say is true. Man is membered into an organism of nerves and senses, a rhythmic organism, and an organism of trunk, limbs and metabolism. These three organisms work together and into one another. We may say that the organism of nerves and senses has its principal activity in the head. But the whole of man is head, after a fashion, functionally. And the same may be said of the other systems. If we take the two outer organisms, that of the nerves and senses and that of the trunk, limbs and metabolic activities, we find an actual opposition between them which is very plainly visible to a spiritual-scientific anatomy and physiology. Say, for example, we are walking. There is *motion* in our limb-organism, movement in space. To this motion there corresponds in a certain portion of our nerves and senses organism, our head organism, a kind of *rest,* proportional to the amount of activity or movement in our limb organism. Please try to understand this correctly. I said: a *proportional* amount of rest. Rest is generally thought of as absolute. A person who is seated, is seated, and people do not notice the degree of intensity with which he sits! This is permissible in ordinary life, where there is no need to make such fine distinctions. But it is not permissible in dealing with the organism of nerves and senses. If we run fast, if our limb organism moves fast, then in our nerves and senses organism there is a stronger desire to be at rest than if we were sauntering along slowly. And everything that happens in our limb organism—or indeed in our metabolic organism, when, for example, the digestive fluids are being kept active by intestinal movements—produces a tendency to rest in our nerves and senses organism. The fact comes to expression externally, as we know.

The head, the principal seat of the nerves and senses organism, is a lazybones compared with the limb organism. It behaves much like a man who sits in a cab and lets himself be drawn along by the horse. The man is at rest; and so does our head sit quietly on the rest of our organism. The head is not even interested if, for instance, I wave my arms! When I wave my left arm, a tendency to rest is set up in the right half of my head. And to this tendency to rest is to be ascribed our ability to accompany our movements with thoughts and ideas. It is quite a mistaken notion of materialistic philosophy that ideas originate from movements in the nerves. On the contrary, if they are ideas about motion in space, they are caused by tendencies to rest in the nervous system. The nervous system quiets down; and because it becomes quiet and abates its vital activities, thoughts find their way into this state of rest and become real for us. Anyone who can look at man with the vision of Spiritual Science and see what happens when he thinks and when ideas occur to him, can never be a materialist, for he knows that in the very same measure that thoughts, in their nature as soul-and-spirit substance, become active and busy—in the same measure do the nerves grow quiet, lose their vitality and energy and even become numb. The nervous system must cease its material activities before it can make room for the soul-and-spirit element of thought. This will help to show us why we have materialism at all. Materialism dates from the time when science no longer understood matter. For material science is characterized by a total inability to conceive the nature of material occurrences, which it therefore endows with a number of non-existent attributes!

So you see there are opposite conditions in man, tending towards equilibrium. Just as there are present at Midsummer natural forces and activities that are directly opposed to those of the depth of Winter, so do we find opposing forces in the human organism, which however hold each other in balance. Yet we shall not think quite correctly about these opposing forces which balance one another until we divide man once more by separating his middle system, the rhythmic system, into two halves, a rhythm of the breath and a rhythm of the blood-circulation—even this discrimination is not absolutely exact, but it is near enough for our purpose —and speak of an upper and lower rhythmic system. Between the upper and lower halves is that part of man which, because it is influenced and permeated from above and below by opposite natural forces, strives most energetically to maintain equilibrium. So that man is divided as it were into two halves, an upper and a lower. The upper half embraces the nerves and senses system which extends, of course, over the whole body. The state of things therefore which I have to picture, is on the one hand a nerves and senses system with a breathing system belonging to it, and on the other hand a trunk, limbs and metabolic system with a circulatory system

176

of the blood belonging to it. These two main systems work in opposite directions and cancel one another.

The organ in man in which the adjustment takes place, in which there is a continual struggle upwards and downwards to maintain equilibrium, is the human heart—which is far from being a pump, as modern physiology would have it, for the purpose of pumping blood through the body! It is, on the contrary, the organ which keeps the upper and lower systems in equilibrium. Therefore even in man's outer physical organism we find an expression of the spiritual events taking place within him, when we observe how Summer and Winter conditions are incessantly offsetting one another within him.

On Earth, Winter can prevail in one region precisely because Summer does not occur at the same time. Otherwise the Summer would balance the Winter, that is to say, there would be neither Winter nor Summer but only equilibrium. This is the real state of things in man. Man is a part of Nature, but since the natural forces oppose each other in his organism they cancel one another and it is as though he were a part of Nature no longer. But for that very reason, man is a *free being*. Natural laws cannot be applied to him, for in him there is not *one* set of natural laws, but two, working against one another, and cancelling each other out. And in this realm where natural forces cancel one another are to be found the soul and spirit of man, unaffected by the working of Nature and only to be recognized in their obedience to the laws of soul and spirit.

From this you can see what a fundamental change of method is necessary when we come to the observation of man, and why a mere application of the external laws of Nature, which are orientated in one direction only, is of no use at all.

But now that we have set before us the true nature of man,

let us see what results follow. We have seen that man cannot be understood unless he is regarded as bearing within him, as it were, a piece of Nature, in such a manner that the counteracting natural forces cancel one another; and if we examine this piece of Nature in man with the eyes of Spiritual Science, we find it to be penetrated as to the physical and etheric bodies during sleep by mineral and vegetable modes of activity, which are seen to be in the Summer condition. If we are now able to observe in the right way this budding, sprouting life, we may learn to understand its real significance.

When does this budding and sprouting take place? When the Ego and astral body are not present, when they are away during sleep. And whence comes this budding and sprouting process? That is precisely what spiritual vision shows us. Let us picture man asleep. His physical and etheric bodies lie in the bed. Spiritual vision sees them as soil, as mineral matter, out of which plant life is sprouting. It is a different form of plant life, of course, from the one we see around us, but recognizable as such by spiritual sight. Above gleam the Ego and astral body like a flame, unable to approach the physical and etheric. Sleeping man therefore is a sort of budding, sprouting plot of ground, with a gleaming Ego and astral body belonging to it, but detached.

And when man is awake? I must describe this state as follows. The mineral and vegetable portions are seen to be withering and collapsing, while the Ego and astral body gleam down into them, and as it were, burn them up. This is walking man, with the mineral matter crumbling within him. The mineral element of man crumbles during his waking hours. There is a sort of plant-like activity which, although quite different in appearance, gives a general and universal impression of autumn foliage, of drooping, withering leaves which are dying and vanishing; and all through this fading substance, big and little flames are gleaming and glowing. These big and little flames are the astral body and the Ego which are now living in the physical and etheric bodies. And then the question arises: What happens to these gleaming and glowing flames during sleep, when they are separated from the physical and etheric bodies?

When this problem is attacked by the methods of occult science we find the solution to be a consequence you could yourselves draw from a comparison of various descriptions that I have given from time to time. The power which drives away the flame and gleam of the Ego and astral body, and which is then actively at work in the budding and sprouting vegetative life of the summer-like, sleeping physical body, and also in its mineral element, causing even that too to evolve a kind of life, so that in the course of its infinitesimal subdividing, it looks like a mass of melting atoms, a continuous mobile mass, everywhere active, fluid-mineral and yet airlike, at all points permeated by sprouting life—what *is* this inner power? It is the reverberating wave of our life before birth, whose pulsations beat upon our physical and etheric bodies during sleep. When we are awake during earthly life we still the pulsating vibrations. So long as the flame and gleam of the Ego and astral body are united with the physical and etheric bodies, we annul those impulses which spring from an existence preceding our earthly life and which we experience during sleep, we bring them to quiescence. And now we learn for the first time, from an inspection of ourselves, how to regard external Nature in the right way. For all natural laws and energies affecting external vegetable and mineral Nature resemble that which is mineral and vegetable in ourselves, permeated with sprouting life, during sleep. And so this means that as our sleep-

179

ing physical and etheric bodies point to our own past, to a spiritual life in which we lived before birth, so does all external Nature that is vegetable or mineral point to a *past*. As a matter of fact, if we are to comprehend aright the natural laws and forces of our external environment, exclusive of the animal element and physical man, we must recognize that they point to the Earth's past, to the dying-away of the Earth. And the thoughts we entertain about external Nature are really directed to the dying element in Earth existence.

Now if this decaying Earth-nature is to be brought to life so that it can receive impulses for the *future,* this can come about in no other way than it does in man, that is to say, by the insertion of soul and spirit into mineral and vegetable. In the case of the animals, the *soul* element enters in, and then with man, *spirit* enters in.

Looked at in this way, the whole world may be said to be divided into two parts. When we look out upon external Nature, in so far as this is mineral and vegetable—and these constitute the principal part of it—we can compare it only with our sleeping physical and etheric organism. When we consider external physical activities, we must admit that all of them depend upon the physical activities in mineral and vegetable matter. Consider the process of nourishment. It begins with the taking in of mineral and vegetable matter. The animal takes it a step further in preparing it as food for man. But all external Nature depends, so far as its physical and etheric activities are concerned, on such an order of things as we find in our sleeping physical and etheric organism. Now in man the Ego and astral organism which we bear within us, and which, during our waking moments while our physical and etheric organism is in its Winter sleep, is in a condition of Summer, being stimulated by the outer senses and the thoughts that form themselves—this Ego and astral organism balances in waking hours the Winter condition of the physical and etheric bodies.

And when we come to apply the methods of Spiritual Science to the cycle of the year, we find in it too a *spiritual Summer* condition belonging to its Winter and a *spiritual Winter* condition belonging to its Summer. These conditions do not, however, balance one another as they do in man. On the contrary, they express themselves in opposite hemispheres, so that on the Earth, physical Winter is strengthened by the Winter of the soul and spirit, and physical Summer by spiritual Summer. Nevertheless these occurrences point to the fact that all surrounding Nature bears within it its past and its future, even as man does.

We have actually the *present* only in waking hours in our physical body in respect to its activities and laws. For during the sleep of our physical and etheric bodies we experience the inworking of a past, a past moreover that was spent in the spiritual world. We find the same thing in the vegetable and mineral worlds as we see them before us and experience their effects upon us. They too are a result of past existence. And they only become present through the Earth being permeated with soul and spirit even as man is. And in the present is contained the germ of the future. But if it is true—and the description I have given you is true—that our physical and etheric organism is an expression of the past precisely when it is independent of the activities of the soul and spirit, then in order to find that which works over into the future we must look to our Ego and astral body; and for the Earth too we must seek the future in that which is spiritual.

Man has evolved to a point when, by help of forces which of course are quite elemental, he has brought the Ego and astral body into companionship with his physical and etheric

181

bodies. The mineral and vegetable world has not yet accomplished this. The Earth's ego and astral body surround
the Earth with soul and spirit but do not permeate her
mineral and vegetable activities. The mineral nature of the
Earth, as observed by us, shows itself unable to let soul and
spirit enter into it, and able only to let them surround it with
light. The vegetable nature shows itself also unable to admit
soul, but in a certain way the upper parts of the plant may
be said to be touched with soul and spirit. Spiritual Science
gives us the following picture of a plant. If I draw it with the
root below, the stem in the middle and the blossom above,
then I have to represent it as in contact with the astral world
through its *blossom*. The astral world does not penetrate the
plant; it merely touches it, and this touching is the origin of
the blossom. The astral substance surrounding the Earth
touches the uppermost portion of the plant, and the flower
appears. I have often spoken of this in an analogy (which
must of course be received with proper delicacy), saying that
the flowering of the plant is the kiss exchanged between the
Sun's light and the plant. It is an astral influence in which
there is no more than a 'touching.'

So that when we look into surrounding Nature, we do not
see in the mineral and vegetable kingdoms exactly what we
see in man. In ourselves as man we behold a mineral nature,
a plant nature, an astral nature and an Ego nature, all belonging to one another. (We will leave the animals out for
the time being and speak of them on some future occasion.)
But we have to see in the mineral and vegetable world themselves that on which physical activity essentially depends.
These worlds show themselves, in external Nature, altogether lacking in astral thought, as well as in self-conscious
spiritual intelligence which is the product of the Ego. The
latter are not to be found in the world outside, neither in the

mineral nor in the plant. For mineral and plant are fundamentally results of the past.

If we observe the Earth's crust and its vegetation aright, we shall look upon all the life of the Earth and say: You crystals, you mountains, you budding and sprouting plants, I see in you monuments of a living, creative past which is now in process of dying. But in man himself, if we are able to have the right insight into this dying element that draws its energy from pre-earthly existence and exhausts itself and dies away in the physical and etheric bodies—in man we see this physical and etheric organism permeated by an astral body and Ego throwing light across into the future and able to unfold freely, on a plane of balanced natural energies, a life of thought and ideation. It may be said that we see in man *past and future side by side.* In Nature on the other hand, so far as she is mineral or vegetable, we see only the past. That element which already functions as future during man's present, is the element that confers *freedom* upon him; and this freedom is not to be found in external Nature. If external Nature were doomed to remain just what her mineral and vegetable kingdoms make her, she would be doomed to die, in the same way that the mere physical and etheric organism of man perishes. Man's physical and etheric organisms die, but man does not, because the nature of the astral and Ego within him carries within it, not death but an *arising,* a *coming into being.*

If therefore external Nature is not to perish, she must be given that which man has through his astral body and his Ego. This means that as man through his astral body and his Ego has self-conscious ideas, he must, in order to ensure a future to the Earth, insert into the Earth too the supersensible and invisible that he has within himself. Even as man must derive his reincarnation in another earth-life from

183

that in him which is supersensible and invisible, since his dying physical and etheric bodies are powerless to confer it, so can no future arise for the Earth from the mineral and vegetable globe that surrounds us. Only when we place into the Earth that which she has not herself, only then can an Earth of the Future arise. And what is not there of itself on the Earth is principally the *active thoughts of man,* as they live and weave in his own Nature-organism, which holds always a balance and is on this account self-dependent. If he brings these independent thoughts to a real existence, he confers a future on the Earth. But he must first have them. Thoughts that we make in our ordinary knowledge of Nature—thoughts about that which is dying away, are mere reflections—not realities. But thoughts we receive from spiritual research are quickened in Imagination, Inspiration, and Intuition. If we accept them they become forms having independent existence in the life of the Earth.

Concerning these creative thoughts I once said in my book entitled *A Theory of Knowledge Implicit in Goethe's World Conception,* that such thinking represents the spiritual form of communion among mankind. For as long as man gives himself up to his mirror-thoughts about external Nature, he does nothing but repeat the past. He lives in corpses of the Divine. When he himself brings life into his thoughts, then, giving and receiving communion through his own being, he allies himself with the element of Divine Spirit which permeates the world and assures its future.

Spiritual knowledge is thus a veritable communion, the beginning of a cosmic ritual that is right and fitting for the man of today, who is then able to grow because he begins to realize how he permeates his own physical and etheric organism with his astral body and Ego, and how, as he quickens the spirit in himself, he charms it also into the dead and dying matter that surrounds him. And a new experience is then his.

When he looks upon his own organism in its *solid* condition, he feels that it links him to the starry universe. In so far as the starry universe is a being at rest, maintaining, e.g. in the signs of the Zodiac a position at rest in relation to the Earth, man is connected in his physical organism with these constellations in space. But by allowing his powers of soul and spirit to pour into this 'form picture' in space, he himself changes the world.

Man is also traversed in like manner by streams of *fluid*. The etheric organism lives in the fluids and juices of the body. It is the etheric body that causes the blood to circulate and that brings into movement the other fluids and juices in man. Through this etheric organism he is brought into touch, if I may so express it, with the *deeds* of the stars, with the *movements* of the planets. Just as the resting pictures in the heaven of the fixed stars act upon, or stand in relation to, the solid structure of the human organism, so do the planetary movements of the system to which we belong stand in relation to the fluids in man.

But as the world presents itself to our immediate vision, it is a dead world. Man transforms it by means of his own spirit, when he shares his spirit with the world, by quickening his thoughts to Imagination, Inspiration, and Intuition, thus fulfilling the spiritual Communion of mankind. It is important that man should become *conscious* of this. The more lively and alert this consciousness becomes, the more easily does man find the way to this spiritual Communion. I should like to give you today some words that may serve as a foundation for this consciousness, words which, when allowed to act rightly upon the soul—and this means, they must be made to live over and over again in the soul until

185

the soul experiences to the full their moving, living meaning
—will then bring something into existence in the human soul
which transforms the dead environment with which man is
connected into a living one, and quickens the past to life in
order that from out of its death may arise the life of the
future. This can only happen when man becomes aware of
his connection with the Cosmos in the following way:

In Earth-activity—(I am imagining the earthly matter
which I take into myself with that which fashions the solid
structure of my organism.)

> In Earth-activity draws near to me,
> Given to me in substance-imaged form,
> The Heavenly Being of the Stars.

For it is a fact that when we take something that serves us
as food and look upon its form, then we find in it a copy
of the constellations of the fixed stars. We take it into ourselves. With the substance of the Earth that is contained in
Earth-activity, we take into us the being of the stars, the
being of the heavens. But we must be conscious that we as
human beings, by a deliberate, loving act of human will,
transform that which has become matter, back again into
spirit. In this manner we perform a real act of *trans-substantiation*. We become aware of our own part in the world
and so the spiritual thought-life is quickened within us.

> In Earth-activity draws near to me,
> Given to me in substance-imaged form,
> The Heavenly Being of the Stars.
> In Willing I see them transformed with Love!

And when we think of that which we take into ourselves
to permeate the fluid part of our organism, the circulation

of the blood and juices, then that, in so far as it originates on Earth, is a copy not of the heavens or of the stars but of the *deeds* of the stars, that is to say, the movements of the planets. And I can become conscious how I spiritualize that, if I stand rightly in the world; and I can speak the following formula:

In Watery life stream into me,
Forming me through with power of substance-force,
The Heavenly Deeds of the Stars—

that is to say, the deeds of the planetary movements. And now:

In Feeling I see them transformed with Wisdom!

While I can see how in *will* the being of the stars changes lovingly into the spiritual content of the future, I can also see how in *feeling* a wise change takes place when I receive into me, in what permeates my fluid organism, a copy of heavenly deeds. Man can experience in this way in his will and in his feeling how he is placed into the world. Surrendering himself to the supreme direction of the universe that is all around him, he can carry out in living consciousness the act of trans-substantiation in the great temple of the Cosmos—standing within it as one who is celebrating a sacrifice in a purely spiritual way.

What would otherwise be mere abstract knowledge achieves a relationship of will and feeling to the world. The world becomes the Temple, the House of God. When man as *knowing* man summons up also powers of *will* and *feeling,* he becomes a sacrificing being. His fundamental relationship to the world rises from knowledge into *cosmic ritual.*

The first beginning of what must come to pass if Anthroposophy is to fulfil its mission in the world is that man's whole relationship to the world must be recognized to be one of cosmic ritual or cult.

I have wished to say this to you, as it were, as a beginning. Next Friday I will speak further about the nature of this ritual in its relation to a real knowledge of Nature. I appointed this lecture for this particular day with a special end in view. For today, when that being of Time which is given in the cycle of the year is brought before our souls, when this year, at any rate for outward perception and experience, comes to an end, we should realize the nature of our relationship to Time—how it rests with us out of the *past* to form and shape the *future,* to work actively for the future, in order to create in the spirit.

One of the poems recited this afternoon began with these words: "Every year finds new graves!" That is profoundly true. But equally true is it that every year finds new cradles. As this year touches the past, so does it also touch the future. And today it is man's first obligation to grasp this future, to reflect that the budding and sprouting life in the external world contains within it the seeds of *death,* and that we must seek for *life* with our *own* power of action. Every New Year is a symbol of this truth. If we see on the one hand the graves, let us behold on the other hand, self-renewing life waiting to receive the seed of the future into itself.

It is our great task this day to observe how in the world around us it is New Year's *Eve*—all is passing and disappearing and dying away; but how in the hearts of men who are conscious of their real manhood, of their divine humanity, there must be the mood of New Year, the mood of the beginning of a new era, of the uprising of new life. Let us not merely turn with a superficial festiveness from a symbolical New Year's Eve to a symbolical New Year's Day;

but let us so turn our thoughts that they may indeed grow powerful and creative, as evolution requires them to be. Let us turn our thoughts away from the dying phenomena which confront us everywhere in modern civilization, like old graves, away from New Year's Eve to New Year's Day, to the day of the Cosmic New Year. But that day will never dawn till man himself decides to bring it to pass.

In Earth-activity draws near to me,
Given to me in substance-imaged form,
The Heavenly Being of the Stars—
In WILLING I see them transformed with love!

In Watery life stream into me,
Forming me through with power of substance-force,
The Heavenly Deeds of the Stars—
In FEELING I see them transformed with Wisdom.

Geistige Kommunion.

Es nahet mir im Erdenwirken,
In Stoffes Abbild mir gegeben,
Der Sterne Himmelswesen:
Ich seh' im Wollen sie sich liebend wandeln.

Es dringen in mich im Wasserleben,
In Stoffes Kraftgewalt mich bildend,
Der Sterne Himmelstaten:
Ich seh' im Fühlen sie sich weise wandeln.

189